The Lord's
PRAYER

THE LORD'S PRAYER

Jesus the Teacher
Jesus the Answer

JEONG WOO "JAMES" LEE

aventine
press

Published by Aventine Press
55 East Emerson St.
Chula Vista CA 91911
www.aventinepress.com

ISBN: 978-1-59330-963-3
Printed in the United States of America

Contents

Acknowledgment

This book is part of our church's 25th Anniversary celebration. Many, especially those who served on our anniversary committee, encouraged me to publish the sermon series I preached on the Lord's Prayer. They found it to be helpful and desired to share it with a larger audience through the medium of this book. So, with a deep sense of humility and gratitude, I have revised the sermons for publication.

I'd like to use this occasion to thank those who made this book possible. First and foremost, I give thanks to God for granting me, chief of sinners, these twenty-five years to minister to the congregation at New Life, La Jolla (PCA). I try not to forget what a great privilege it is to shepherd "the church of God, which he obtained with his own blood" (Acts 20:28). Who is adequate for this work (2 Cor. 2:16)? But since my adequacy comes from God (2 Cor. 3:5), I'll continue to rely on the Lord to do what is possible only through Him (Phil. 4:13).

I also would like to thank the congregation of New Life, La Jolla. What a blessing it is to minister to a congregation, who desire to hear the Word of God faithfully preached rather than to have their ears tickled with the wisdom of the world! If we have a multi-ethnic but mono-cultural (which is Christian and biblical) congregation, it is because you love the gospel of Jesus Christ, which transcends whatever differences that divide and antagonize people. Thank you for encouraging me to preach the whole counsel of God without any compromise. I'd like to express my deep gratitude especially to Richard and Esther Kim, who have been with me all these twenty-five years. Thank you for your friendship and loyalty.

I'd like to thank our elders—Joel Norris, Rich Carlson, and Bill Honaker—my fellow shepherds at New Life. I'm so thankful that I can come out of our session meetings energized and motivated rather than drained and beaten down. Thank you for the love and respect with which you speak even when we disagree. Thank you for your firm confidence in the truth of God's Word and your unswerving commitment to apply it to the shepherding of Christ's church.

I'd like to thank our deacons—Lynn Roberts, Paul Han, Joseph Boyd, Edwin Sumargo—for their example of faithful and joyful service even though it is not noticed and appreciated as much as it should be. I trust that "your Father who sees in secret will reward you" (Matt. 6:4). Thank you for encouraging us to grow into a community of love and service by your example of diligent and sacrificial service!

I also would like to thank our 25th Anniversary Committee members—Elizabeth Roberts, Young Chang, Karly Eberts, Siew Brown, Josh Kim and Sheri Carlson. Thank you for planning all the activities throughout this past year and helping us celebrate

God's faithfulness to our congregation. I'd like to especially thank Young Chang for his constant encouragement to get this book done and for his patience with my slow progress.

I'd like to also thank my family. Thank you, Audrey and Connor, for making having two teenagers at home so much more fun and enjoyable than we expected! And thank you, Averey, for bringing so much laughter to Mommy and Daddy and making our lives so much more exciting in more ways than one. And my big thanks to Cassie, my dear wife. Thank you for your constant sacrifice and labor for our family. Thank you for the warmth and love with which you care for the members of our congregation. Thank you for your understanding and patience with me and your wise counsel. "An excellent wife who can find? She is far more precious than jewels" (Prov. 31:10). I thank God for granting me a truly excellent wife!

And last, but not least, I'd like to thank my oldest daughter, Audrey, for going over the manuscript to make corrections and suggestions. I cannot believe that my tiny little firstborn has grown up enough to edit Daddy's sermons! Thank you for your labor!

I pray that the Lord would be pleased to use this small book to show the surpassing value of knowing Jesus Christ.

September, 2019
La Jolla, California

Introduction to the Lord's Prayer

The prayer in Matt. 6:9-13 is known as the Lord's Prayer. Why it is called by that name is obvious: it is taught by our Lord Jesus Christ. But in this short book, I would like to suggest that there is another important reason for the title. *It should be called the Lord's Prayer because the Lord Jesus Christ is the ultimate answer to all the petitions of the prayer.*

This should not surprise us. What is the greatest blessing we can ever hope to receive? What is the ultimate fulfillment of God's covenant promises to His people? Paul said, "For all the promises of God find their Yes in [Jesus Christ]" (2 Cor. 1:20a; unless specified, all Scripture quotations are from ESV). He is the Offspring of the woman, who vanquished the serpent of old (Gen. 3:15). He is the Seed of Abraham, in whom all the families of the earth are blessed (Gen. 12:3). He is our Passover (1 Cor. 5:7), "the Lamb of God, who takes away the sin of the world" (John 1:29). He is the Prophet like Moses (Deut. 18:15) yet greater than Moses: "For the law was given through Moses; grace and truth came through Jesus Christ" (John 1:17). He is the true High Priest according to the order of Melchizedek (Ps. 110:4) through whom we enter the heavenly sanctuary (Heb. 9:11-12). He is David's greater Son—the Son of God, indeed!—who will build a house of God's eternal dwelling among His people and the throne of whose kingdom will be forever (2 Sam. 7:13). The list goes on and on.

Since the Lord's Prayer is directly taught by the Lord Himself, we can safely assume that it is the noblest and loftiest of all prayers. As such, it cannot ask for anything less than the absolute best. What is the absolute best if not the Lord of heaven and earth, the Fount of life and every blessing, the Redeemer of His people, the Way and the Truth and the Life? So, as we take a look at the various petitions in the Lord's Prayer, we will see how each of them finds its ultimate answer and fulfillment in the Teacher of this prayer Himself! The thesis of this book is startlingly simple. But I hope you can already see its profound and far-reaching ramifications in our salvation and life.

The Lord's Prayer and Jesus' Ministry

We have many accounts of Jesus' commitment to prayer. His ministry began with prayer. After the baptism, before He officially launched His public ministry, He spent forty days and nights in the wilderness, fasting. The Bible makes it clear that He was there to undergo Satan's temptation (Matt. 4:1). But it is hard to conceive that Jesus simply fasted without praying. Jesus did not go into the wilderness just to skip meals; He went there to pray in preparation for His ministry. Fasting, Jesus engaged in an intense form of prayer during His wilderness days.

Prayer played an important role at the end of Jesus' public ministry as well. Right before He was crucified, He went to the Garden of Gethsemane and prayed the most agonizing prayer in His earthly life. Three times He prayed, "My Father, if it be possible, let this cup pass from me; nevertheless, not as I will, but as you will" (Matt. 26:39). And how can we forget His heart-wrenching prayer of lamentation on the cross: "My God, My God, why have you forsaken Me?" And His very last words were words of prayer: "Father, into your hands I commit my spirit!"

We are also told that it was customary for Jesus to go away alone to pray during His public ministry (Luke 5:16). We even have a few records of Jesus' prayer—most prominently in John 17 ("Jesus' High Priestly Prayer") but also before the tomb of Lazarus (John 11:41-42) and before He gave the invitation to come to Him for rest (Matt. 11:25-27), etc.

Not only did Jesus pray, He also taught about prayer on many occasions—how to pray and what *kind* of things to pray for. But the Lord's Prayer is the only instance of Jesus teaching His disciples what exactly to pray for. Why did He teach them this prayer? His purpose was not to give them some magical chants to recite for protection and luck, as so many prayers are in other religions. Why, then?

It is helpful to see the occasion on which another version of the Lord's Prayer is given in Luke 11:2-4. There, the occasion was the disciples' request: "Lord, teach us to pray, as John taught his disciples" (Luke 11:1). Some commentators have noted that, in Israel at that time, a prayer was to a religious movement what a slogan is to a political campaign these days ("Make America Great Again", for example). This seems to be what is reflected in the disciples' words, "Lord, teach us to pray, *as John taught his disciples.*" John, too, had a prayer for his followers, it seems. Having seen that, and having seen other movements, the disciples wanted Jesus to define His ministry with a prayer. Anyone hearing or reciting this prayer should know what Jesus' ministry was all about.

The Lord's Prayer and Its Location in the Sermon on the Mount

The Sermon on the Mount is about the kingdom of heaven. This is made evident by the way the Sermon on the Mount begins. It begins with the Beatitudes and the Beatitudes begin with the kingdom of heaven: "Blessed are the poor in spirit, for theirs is *the kingdom of heaven*" (5:3). The middle section of the Sermon on the Mount (5:21-7:23), which makes up the bulk of the sermon, is bracketed by Jesus' words concerning one's entrance into the kingdom of heaven: "For I tell you, unless your righteousness exceeds that of the scribes and Pharisees, you will never enter *the kingdom of heaven*" (Matthew 5:20); "Not everyone who says to me, 'Lord, Lord,' will enter the kingdom of heaven, but the one who does the will of my Father who is in heaven" (Matthew 7:21). So then, the Sermon on the Mount is thoroughly concerned with the life in the kingdom of heaven.

The Lord's Prayer (6:9-13) is found at the center of the Sermon on the Mount (Chs. 5-7). This shows how important prayer is to the life in the kingdom of heaven. In fact, Jesus dedicates a whole chapter (Ch. 6) to the teaching of prayer (except vv. 1-4). This is one third of His entire sermon! As the sons of Seth were characterized as a people of prayer, who called upon the name of the Lord (Gen. 4:26), so are those, who belong to the kingdom of heaven: they are a people of prayer, whose eyes look longingly toward heaven, where God is seated in His glorious throne; they are a people, in whose life prayer takes a central position.

The Lord's Prayer and Our Prayer

This is how Jesus introduces the Lord's Prayer: "Pray, *then*, in this way…" (6:9a). Pay attention to the particle, "then." It connects the Lord's Prayer with what Jesus taught in the preceding section. Here, Jesus teaches the Lord's Prayer as the alternative to what He taught the disciples not to do in prayer. They are not to be like the hypocrites, praying in the public to be seen by men (6:5). Rather, they are to pray in the inner room because they are praying to their Father, who sees in secret (6:4). And when they pray, they are not to use meaningless repetition as the Gentiles do, thinking that they will be heard for their many words (6:7). So, Jesus gives the Lord's Prayer as an example of how His people ought to pray.

You will notice, then, that the Lord's Prayer is short and concise. This doesn't mean that our prayer should not last longer than a minute at a time. What Jesus spoke against was not how long or how short we pray; He spoke against meaningless repetitions, against using many words to be heard. Sometimes we pray long because we think that God won't hear us unless our prayers are long. So, we say the same things again and again; we use many words to fill up the time. Prayer thus becomes a work to earn God's favor. Jesus abhors such an attitude, such lack of trust in God. Jesus says, "[Y]our Father knows what you need, before you ask Him" (6:8b).

But I dare say that Jesus, who opposes repetitive, verbose prayers, is equally opposed to short prayers that are merely mechanical. We often pray only to fulfill the bare minimum of our religious obligation, especially when there is no big crisis in our life. Then our prayer becomes short and concise for all the wrong reasons because we don't really care. What God hates is a heartless prayer. We can pray a heartless prayer both in long prayers as well as in short prayers.

This leads us to the question of proper use of the Lord's Prayer. We should use it as our prayer but it is not the only prayer we are allowed to pray. It is given also as an example, after which we should pattern our own prayers.

In praying this prayer, we should be careful not to use it as a mindless chant or a magical incantation. Other religions have incantations, which they believe have magical powers to ward off demons and bad luck. They need not know what they are saying—these incantations may be in a foreign language or an archaic dialect. All they need to do is say the right words and make the right sounds and they will work their charm, they believe. Such is not the intended use of the Lord's Prayer. This prayer calls for our proper understanding of what we utter. It calls for our whole-hearted agreement with what we say. It calls for our will and desire to be conformed to what it petitions. This cannot be done by mindless repetitions of the prayer.

The Structure of the Lord's Prayer

The Lord's Prayer is divided into two sections: the invocation and the petitions. The invocation is, of course, "Our Father in heaven." The petition section is what follows and is further divided into two sections: what J. Jeremias calls the "Thou-petitions" (which I will call "Your-petitions" for the "modern" ear) and the "we-petitions" (which I will call "Us-petitions" to reflect the actual word used in the Lord's Prayer).

The first section of petitions ("Your-petitions") is concerned with the things that pertain to God: "hallowed be *Your name*"; "*Your kingdom* come"; "*Your will* be done, on earth as it is in heaven." The second set of petitions ("Us-petitions") is concerned with the things that pertain to us: "give *us* this day *our* daily bread"; "forgive *us our* debts, as we also have forgiven our debtors"; "lead *us* not into temptation, but deliver *us* from evil."

The order of these two sections is important. First, this order shows the primacy of God and His glory. This is important for us to remember as we bring our petitions to God, isn't it? In our desperate need, it is easy for us to think of God merely as a cosmic Butler, who is there to help us if we ask Him earnestly and urgently enough. This is how most of other religions view prayer. It is a way to get what the supplicants wants. It is preceded or accompanied by many rituals and sacrifices to appease their god(s) or get their attention. Why? So the god(s) would be persuaded to answer their prayers. The spirit of such prayer can be summarized as "Not your will but my will be done." Crudely speaking, the religious rituals and sacrifices can be seen as a means of manipulating the gods to do what the petitioners want.

But God doesn't exist for us: we exist for Him. This should be obvious. There was when we did not exist. But there was never when God did not exist: He is the One who was and is and ever will be, who brought all things into being, including man. And after He made all things, He surveyed everything and declared that it was very good (Gen 1:31). This shows how God made all things for His glory and pleasure, especially man. So, Paul commands the Corinthians, "So, whether you eat or drink, or whatever you do, do all to the glory of God" (1 Cor. 10:31). The Westminster Shorter Catechism reflects this idea when it says, "The chief end of man is to glorify God and to enjoy Him forever" (A. 1). As exemplified in our Lord's most heart-felt prayer in the Garden of Gethsemane, the spirit of the Christian prayer is, "Not my will but Your will be done." We should not be surprised that the Lord's Prayer reflects this theme in its order of petitions. God's glory and kingdom should be the primary concern of our prayers, not our own desires and needs.

But "primary" doesn't mean "exclusive." The Lord's Prayer does not just consist of "Your-petitions"; it also consists of "Us-petitions." How thankful we should be that our Lord does not dismiss our concerns as unimportant or irrelevant! This prayer shows that He cares about our needs. In fact, it shows that God's glory and the meeting of our needs are connected with each other, inseparably so. After all, God is called "our *Father*." Later on in the Sermon on the Mount, our Lord says, "If you then, who are evil, know how to give good gifts to your children, how much more will your Father who is in heaven give good things to those who ask him" (Matt. 7:11)!

This sheds some light on the significance of the order of these petitions. This particular order shows that God's care for our needs flows out of God's primary care for His glory. This may sound dishonorable—if God cares for us for *His* own glory, what honor is there? Isn't this selfish? That kind of reasoning may be applied to us but not to God, as John Piper showed. For God is the absolute, ultimate Good. If being virtuous is loving that which is good and seeking the greatest good above all else, then a good God is morally obligated to love and seek that which is the greatest good. And since He is the ultimate Good, He must seek His glory above all things: "the chief end of God is to enjoy glorifying himself."[1]

Here is why this is good news for us. Since God is almighty, He will not fail to glorify Himself. And if His glory is inseparably connected to our good by virtue of His covenant with us, we have an unshakable assurance that He will take care of us without fail. This is guaranteed for us not only by God's unchangeable and infallible character but also by Jesus' work of redemption on our behalf. So, we should be bold in our prayers and confident in our expectations.

---

[1] John Piper, "Is God for Us or for Himself" (https://www.desiringgod.org/messages/is-god-for-us-or-for-himself--2).

But what could be our boldest prayer? Is it not to pray for the greatest blessing of all, which is to have God as our portion and inheritance? And isn't that the summation of all of God's promises? "For all the promises of God find their Yes in him. That is why it is through him that we utter our Amen to God for his glory" (2 Cor. 1:20). And that is precisely what is reflected in the Lord's Prayer: Jesus Christ is the ultimate answer to all of its petitions.

"Our Father in Heaven"
(Jesus, God's Son)

"Our Father"
Too Familiar?

Some of us have prayed the Lord's Prayer hundreds of times. Every time we recite the Lord's Prayer, we begin as Jesus taught us, "Our Father in heaven...." So, we are used to it. There is nothing new or surprising about addressing God as "Our Father in heaven...." Of course God is our heavenly Father!

But has this always been the case? When Jesus taught this prayer, how was it received by the Jews of that time, or by the Gentile converts? People were often astonished by His teaching. That was the case when He preached the Sermon on the Mount (Matt. 7:28). There was something new about His teaching (e.g., Matt 5:21-22, "You have heard that it was said to those of old.... But I say to you..."). His teaching was new not because He contradicted the Scriptures (which at that time consisted only of the Old Testament). Jesus said, "I have not come to abolish [the Law or the Prophets] but to fulfill them" (Matt. 5:17). You see, the newness of His teaching sprang from the fact that the kingdom of heaven was final at hand (Matt. 3:2), which was the message with which He began His ministry! The age of fulfillment had arrived in *His* coming into this world!

God as Israel's "Father"

There was something radical about the way Jesus was telling His disciples to address God. Not that God was never called "Father" in the Old Testament. But "God is seldom spoken of as 'Father' in the Old Testament, in fact only fifteen times."[2] And when God was called "Father," it was used as a metaphor, or in a simile, to liken God as a father. In Isa. 64:8, for example, God's fatherhood to Israel is likened to the relationship between the potter and the clay. What is in view here is the relationship between the Creator and His creatures. The potter making clay vessels is obviously an analogy for God's creation of man. In other instances, too, God is addressed as Israel's Father because He is their Redeemer ("For you are our Father, though Abraham does not know us, and Israel does not acknowledge us; you, O LORD, are *our Father, our Redeemer* from of old is your name," Isa. 63:16) and Lord ("I said, How I would set you among my sons, and give you a pleasant land, a heritage most beautiful of all nations. And I thought you would call me, My Father, and would not turn from *following me…*," Jer. 3:19), etc.

God was *like* a father to the Israelites because He created them and brought them into being. God was *like* a father to them because He delivered them from the Egyptian bondage and established them as a new nation. God was *like* a father to them because He cared for them with love, patience, instruction, and guidance,

---

2 Johachim Jeremias, *The Prayers of Jesus* (Philadelphia: Fortress Press, 1978), p. 12.

sustaining and protecting them. What an awesome privilege it was for the Israelites to know that the almighty God cared for them—affectionately, patiently, gently, and firmly like a father cares for his children!

We can safely assume that the Jewish perception of God as their Father remained in the realm of metaphor and simile. To think any more than that would be beyond their wildest religious imagination. So, when Jesus taught people to address God as "Our father in heaven…," there was nothing so radical about the idea per se.

God as the Father of Jesus Christ

So then, in what way was Jesus' teaching radical?

We all have experienced how the same thing can sound different depending on who says it. Every parent has to laugh at one point because his child finally accepts what he has been telling her because somebody else told her. Similarly, many people may offer words of comfort to a person struggling with depression or anxiety. They may even say the same thing. But the same words have so much more impact if they come from someone who went through the same problem.

This teaching to call God "our Father in heaven" comes from the One, who consistently addressed God as "My Father." Was that anything special? God did address *the nation of Israel* as His son (Ex. 4:22; Hos. 11:1). But God did not address any *one individual* as such, except the messianic figure (Ps. 2:7, 2 Sam. 7:14). What is more, it was one thing for God to call anyone His son; it was quite another for a person to call God "my Father." So, after surveying the biblical as well as the extra-biblical literature up to the time of Jesus, Jeremias concluded, "there is as yet no evidence in the literature of ancient Palestinian Judaism that 'my Father' is used as a personal address to God."[3]

Some question Jeremias' methodology in arriving at this conclusion. Indeed, God does say in Jer. 3:4-5, "Have you not just now called to me, 'My father, you are the friend of my youth—will he be angry forever, will he be indignant to the end?'" But here, God is not speaking of any one individual but of Israel as a whole. (The same is true of Jer. 3:19). The only instance of an individual personally addressing God as "my Father" would be Ps. 89:26. There we read, "He shall cry to me, 'You are my Father, my God, and the Rock of my salvation.'" As you can see, this was a prophecy, something yet to be done. And the person in view was the Seed of David, the promised Messiah who was yet to come. This passage (along with Ps. 2:7 and 2 Sam. 7:14, in which God addresses the messianic figure as "My Son") points to one of the unique features of the promised Messiah: He would address God personally as "my Father."

And this is exactly what Jesus did all throughout His ministry. In the Gospel of Matthew alone, Jesus addresses God as "my Father" thirteen times. This was far from ordinary. Consider how the religious leaders responded. They saw it as a blasphemy (John 10:29-33). They would have been right—except that this was Jesus.

Jesus was no ordinary person. He was conceived by the Holy Spirit (Matt. 1:18, 20). The angel told Mary when he announced her virgin conception by the Holy Spirit, "He will be great and will be called *the Son of the Most High*. And the Lord God will give to him the throne of his father David" (Luke 1:32). When

---

3 Jeremias, p. 29

Jesus returned from Egypt, it is said to be the fulfillment of the prophecy, "Out of Egypt I called *my son*" (Hos. 11:1; Matt. 2:15). When He was just twelve, He referred to the temple as "My Father's house." And of course, when Jesus was baptized by John the Baptist at the Jordan, "a voice from heaven said, 'This is my beloved Son, with whom I am well pleased'" (Matt. 3:17). Add to this the supernatural, miraculous works Jesus performed.

In what sense is Jesus God's Son? He is God's only begotten, eternal Son (John 1:1-3; 3:16). It was this eternal Son of God who was teaching—indeed, commanding(!)—His disciples to address God as "our Father".

Jesus' Divine Sonship and Our Adoption

But what difference does this make? Can God be our Father any more than in the same metaphoric sense? Not simply by Jesus' command, of course. Jesus did so much more than just give a command. We read in Galatians 4:4-6,

> "But when the fulness of the time came, God sent forth His Son, born of a woman, born under the Law, in order that He might redeem those who were under the Law, that we might receive the adoption as sons. And because you are sons, God has sent forth the Spirit of His Son into our hearts, crying, 'Abba! Father!'"

Notice the exchange. The eternal Son of God comes, born of a woman, born under the Law, so that those who are born of women, born under the Law, might receive the adoption as sons. The Son of God bound Himself by a covenant to those who are under the Law so that those who are under the Law might stand with the Son of God as God's sons. (We use the word "sons" here because the idea of Old Testament inheritance is associated with sons. Indeed, Paul goes on to say in the next verse, "Therefore you are no longer a slave, but a son; and if a son, then an heir through [the gracious act of] God.")

What is in view here is our adoption as God's children. This is no longer just a metaphor as in the Old Testament. Our adoption is in Jesus Christ, through our (covenantal and mystical) union with the true, eternal Son of God. Of course, if Israel was God's son in any sense—metaphorical or otherwise—it was ultimately on account of Jesus Christ. As the Levitical priesthood and the sacrificial system looked forward to their fulfillment in Jesus Christ as our true High Priest and the Lamb of God; as the temple served as a picture of Jesus Christ, the true Temple; as the Davidic monarchy was but a vehicle through which the true King should come, who is David and Solomon's greater Son, Israel's sonship to God in the Old Testament was a shadow of our adoption as sons *in Jesus Christ*. Because of the coming of Christ, we now understand more fully and clearly the glories of our adoption as God's children.

In our adoption as God's children, we do not become divine, of course. But insofar as we are united with Jesus Christ, who is the true, eternal Son of God, we are the sons of God in a real way, though mystical. Regarding our adoption, Horatius Bonar said,

"Thus a new relationship was established, such as till then could never have been conceived of as even possible. The tie of creation, though not dissolved, was now to be lost in the closer, dearer tie of kindred.... Thus the saints are the nearest kinsman of the Son of God; and if of the Son, then of the Father also, as He hath said, 'I and my Father are one,' 'believest thou not that I am in the Father, and the Father in me?'"[4]

4 Horatius Bonar, *The Night of Weeping and the Morning of Joy* (Pensacola: Mount

God's Love for Us in His Son

So then, God does not love us merely as the paragon of His creation. God does not love us merely as His own redeemed people, the chosen subjects of His kingdom. He loves us as His dear children with the love with which He loves His only begotten Son, who is in the bosom of the Father! For we have been united with Jesus Christ and now our lives are hidden with Him in God (Col. 3:3)! This is the glory of our redemption. Through the only begotten God (John 1:18), we have been allowed to take part in the inner-Trinitarian love between the Father and the Son! Without becoming God, we have been allowed (as much as creatures can be allowed) to enjoy the benefit and joy of the love between God the Father and God the Son! This is the reality we take hold of when we pray, "Our Father in heaven!" Oh, who can fathom the depth of this mystery?

This is why one of the favorite titles of God in the New Testament is "the God and Father of our Lord Jesus Christ" (Rom. 15:6; 2 Cor. 1:3; Eph. 1:3; 1 Pet. 1:3). Consider how this title replaces one of the favorite titles of God in the Old Testament—"God of Abraham, Isaac, and Jacob." Do you see the implication?

Why did the Old Testament saints cherish the divine title, the God of Abraham, Isaac, and Jacob? In calling upon God by that title, they were invoking God's gracious covenant with the Patriarchs. In so doing, they were also expressing their longing to share in the intimacy the Patriarchs enjoyed in their covenant relationship with God.

Think about what it means for us to address God as "the God and Father of our Lord Jesus Christ." (This is at the background

Zion Publications), p. 13

of "Our Father in heaven" in the Lord's Prayer.) We are no longer simply invoking God's gracious covenant with the Patriarchs. Rather, we are invoking God's covenant with Jesus Christ—both the foundation and fulfillment of God's covenant with Abraham, Isaac, and Jacob! When we invoke this New Testament title of God, we are expressing our longing to share in the intimacy our Lord Jesus Christ enjoys in His inner-Trinitarian relationship with the Father! And this longing is not something we came up with on our own. It is stirred up by the gracious invitation of the Son of God Himself! So then, we have the assurance that this longing of ours will be satisfied in God's fatherly love for, and care of, us as His beloved children!

"In Heaven"
God our Father and the Kingdom of God

Why is this privilege of intimacy with God so great? Because God is so great. God is not simply "our Father." He is "our Father *in heaven*." We must not lose sight of this truth, this tension. That Jesus teaches us to address God as "our Father" is both shocking and not so shocking at the same time. It is shocking because the central focus of Jesus' Sermon on the Mount is the *kingdom* of God, in which God is *King*. Do you remember how Jesus began the sermon? "Blessed are the poor in spirit, for theirs is *the kingdom of heaven*" (5:3). In fact, the kingdom of heaven was the central motif of Jesus' proclamation all through His public ministry. He inaugurated His official ministry by proclaiming, "Repent, for *the kingdom of heaven* is at hand" (4:17)! Yet, we are to address the King of heaven as our *Father*.

Indeed, there is another strand, which is woven throughout the Sermon on the Mount—an undeniable emphasis on God as our Father. Just to give you an idea, the word "God" is used only five times in the Sermon on the Mount. The word "Lord" is used also five times but four of them occur in two verses (7:21, 22), each of which has the same phrase, "Lord, Lord." Compare that to the seventeen times Jesus mentions God as Father in one way or the other: "your Father who is in heaven," five times; "your heavenly Father," four times; "your Father," seven times; and "My Father who is in heaven," once. The proliferation of this image of God as our heavenly Father is quite striking. And this is indeed a unique feature of the New Testament.

In the Sermon on the Mount, there is a healthy tension between the awesome magnificence of God as the King and Lord of heaven and earth and the intimate closeness of God as our Father. That tension is wonderfully present in this invocation. In teaching us to call God "our Father," Jesus affirms our new intimacy with God. Even so, in teaching us to address God as "our Father *in heaven*," He does not allow us to lose sight of God's transcendent majesty. The two must not be separated. God's intimate, fatherly love toward us is wonderful because He is so magnificent and unmatched in His glory.

How wonderful this message is! God is God and He is not to be mocked. If He is to be worthy of our worship and service, He must be supreme in his majesty and glory far beyond whatever dignity we may have as human beings. But how crushing and forbidding His weight of glory would be if He did not deign to be our heavenly Father! Because our union with Jesus Christ, the eternal Son of God, we can enjoy an intimate relationship with the almighty God.

What's in a Title?

Throughout this study on the Lord's Prayer, I will try to show how important each petition is. But I cannot stress enough the importance of how we begin this prayer. You and I know how easy it is for us to begin our prayer mindlessly. We all have a habitual (and I fear, mindless) way of starting our prayers— "Dear Lord," "Dear heavenly Father," "Dear God," etc. When we address God in such a mindless way, great is our loss. Many of you know the acronym for prayer: A-C-T-S—Adoration, Confession, Thanksgiving, and Supplication. It is so easy for us to jump to our supplications right away, especially when we are faced with heavy trials. Why should we begin our prayer with adoration? By calling out the names and titles of God, we are to remind ourselves of whom we are dealing with, whom we are bringing our petitions to.

If we do more than just mindlessly call out God's name, if we can only remember that the almighty God of heaven and earth is our Father in heaven, most of our prayers will be answered right there and then, simply in the renewed appreciation of who our heavenly Father is. If the almighty God is our heavenly Father, whom shall we fear, of what shall we be afraid? This truth can calm the raging storm of fear in our hearts, no matter how strong. Our heavenly Father loves us more than we love ourselves. He knows what is best for us better than we do. He even knows what we need even before we ask. He always has our best interest in mind. Of whom can we say such a thing without any tinge of doubt? What is more, God is *able* to do what is best for us! Whenever we pray, whenever we call out to God as our heavenly Father, we have an opportunity to glory in this amazing privilege and joy!

Yet, how is that possible for sinners like us? It certainly is not on account of our own goodness and merit, which are like filthy rags. It is only because of the eternal Son of God, who came into this world as the Son of Man, born of the woman, born under the law, in the weakness of our flesh, subjecting Himself to the curse of the law on our behalf, bearing the punishment of our sin in our place. By His punishment, we are forgiven; by His wounds, we are healed; by His weakness, we are made strong; by His obedience, we are declared righteous; in the likeness of His Holy Spirit conception, we are born of the Spirit; by His incarnation as the Son of Man, we are made sons and daughters of God. We cannot even begin to pray the Lord's Prayer without Christ and His work of redemption. For we cannot address God as our heavenly Father without being united to the Son of God.

Don't Forget to Pray Together

As we conclude, let me briefly mention the importance of calling out to God as "*our* Father in heaven." Matthew Henry says that this title teaches us "that we must pray, not only alone and for ourselves, but with and for others; for we are members one of another, and are called into fellowship with each other." Let us seek to pray not only for one another in our private prayers but also *with* another! This should be done in our worship service but not just there only. Let us seek opportunities to pray with one another in our family devotions and in our weekly gatherings, both formal and informal. Let us encourage one another by praying with one another! Let us rejoice together that God is our heavenly Father in our Lord Jesus Christ!

"Hallowed be Your Name"
(Jesus, the Vindicator of God's Name)

What are We Asking for?

"Hallowed be Your name." This is the first petition of the Lord's Prayer and it is a difficult one. To start with, the word used here is not a common word we use these days. What does "hallowed" mean? To hallow something is to sanctify something, to make something holy. To be hallowed, then, is to be made holy. In this petition, we are praying that God would make His name holy.

This raises an immediate question: does this mean that God's name is not holy? If something must be made holy, it cannot in a state of holiness. But it's ridiculous to think that God's name is not holy. Even in this world, there are certain things we hold to be "sacred"—such as our marriage vow, trust between parents and children or between clergy and parishioners, our statements under oath, etc. If so, how much more sacred is the name of God? If there is anything at all that is holy, or sacred, it is the name of God. For God is holy: He is the Essence of holiness, the Source of whatever is holy and sacred.

So then, there is something baffling about this petition. On the one hand, we know that God's name is holy—in fact, it is the most sacred thing of all. On the other hand, this petition seems to suggest that God's name is not holy in some sense. How can this be?

God and His Name

We must distinguish between God and His name. While the two are inseparably connected—try to separate you and your name— the two still need to be distinguished—your name (i.e., the particular alphabetical arrangement that spells your name) is not you in person. We can say that "God" refers to the essence and fullness of His being—God as He is in and of Himself. "God's name," on the other hand, represents that by which He is known. This idea of being known presupposes the existence of other beings, to whom God is known through His name.

But we need to make another distinction: the name of God, which is inherently holy; the name of God which is perceived as holy by others. Now we can see in what sense God's holy name can be defiled. The inherent sanctity of God's name cannot be defiled in any way. The only possible way is how the name of God may be *perceived* by moral creatures like men or angels. Such a possibility can exist, of course, only in the context of the Fall and sin. For a moral creature who is good and untainted by sin cannot see God's holiness as anything other than what it is—holy—and thus worthy of our utmost reverence and sincerest worship.

God's Name Profaned?

It is not difficult to see, then, that the name of God is profaned in the fallen world in the perception of sinners. Many do not honor and worship God as He ought to be as their God, their

Maker, their Sustainer, and their Benefactor, by whose goodness and generosity they enjoy everything they have. They deny God's existence and His work. They make mockery of those that believe in God.

When we consider the fallen condition of this world, we can sense the urgency of this petition. We cannot deny the painful recognition that the world has gone haywire; it is not the way it ought to be. This is no news. Everyone recognizes it. Everyone knows that the world is not the way it should be—though everyone has a different idea of how and why. This petition points to the essence of all the problems in the world—man's unwillingness to acknowledge the holiness of God and worship Him. What it means to acknowledge God's holiness, the Westminster Larger Catechism explains:

> "In the first petition (which is, Hallowed be thy name,) acknowledging the utter inability and indisposition that is in ourselves and all men to honour God aright, we pray, that God would by his grace enable and incline us and others to know, to acknowledge, and highly to esteem him, his titles, attributes, ordinances, word, works, and whatsoever he is pleased to make himself known by; and to glorify him in thought, word, and deed: that he would prevent and remove atheism, ignorance, idolatry, profaneness, and whatsoever is dishonourable to him; and, by his overruling providence, direct and dispose of all things to his own glory" (A. 177).

It is abundantly clear that the fallen man does not, and cannot, properly acknowledge and honor the sanctity of God's holy name.

Why Jesus Taught This Prayer

It is obvious why Jesus is teaching us to pray this prayer. God is holy, three times holy (Isa. 6:3, Rev. 4:8). But Jesus saw all around Him that God was not held in highest esteem. He lamented that what Isaiah complained of the people of Israel was still true: "This people honors me with their lips, but their heart is far from me; in vain do they worship me, teaching as doctrines the commandments of men" (Matt. 15:8). He was enraged that the temple had become "a den of robbers" instead of a house of prayer (Matt. 21:13). How He must have desired that the holy name of His Father should be restored in the hearts and lives of His people!

But Jesus did not invent this petition merely out of His zeal for the name of His Father. He knew more than anyone that we should pray according to God's will. (In fact, later in the Lord' Prayer He taught His disciples to pray, "Your will be done, on earth as it is in heaven.") Even in the Garden of Gethsemane, where He cried out to God to pass the cup of wrath from Him— not just once but three times!—He concluded each time with these words of total surrender to His Father's will: "nevertheless, not as I will, but as you will" (Matt. 26:39). We can assume, then, that this petition is rooted in God's will.

When God's Name was Most Profaned

Indeed, we notice that this petition reflects what God declared to do a long time ago, particularly through the Prophet Ezekiel:

> "Son of man, when the house of Israel lived in their own land, they defiled it by their ways and their deeds. Their ways before me were like the uncleanness of a woman in her menstrual impurity. So I poured out my wrath upon

them for the blood that they had shed in the land, for the idols with which they had defiled it. I scattered them among the nations, and they were dispersed through the countries. In accordance with their ways and their deeds I judged them. But when they came to the nations, wherever they came, *they profaned my holy name*, in that people said of them, 'These are the people of the LORD, and yet they had to go out of his land" (Ezek. 36:17-20).

You see what is going on here. On account of Israel's blatant disobedience and persistent rebellion against Him, God finally drove the Jews out of the Promised Land and scattered them among the nations by the hand of Babylon. This was precisely according to the terms of the covenant God established with Israel at Mount Sinai through Moses. The Lord swore by His holy name,

> "And it shall come about [if you disobey] that as the LORD delighted over you to prosper you, and multiply you, so the LORD will delight over you to make you perish and destroy you; and you shall be *torn from the land* where you are entering to possess it. Moreover, the LORD will *scatter* you among all peoples, from one end of the earth to the other end of the earth..." (Deut. 28:63-64a).

In driving out the people of Israel from the Promised Land, God was being faithful to His covenant with them.

But that was not how the nations *perceived* it. They jeered at the Jews and their God, Jehovah. You see, to the ancient, polytheistic mind, the fate of a people reflected the power of their god(s). If a nation was victorious, it was because its god was stronger than the god of its enemy nation. The defeat of a nation meant the defeat of its god (cf., 2 Kings 18:32-35). Such was the humiliation that God suffered when the people of Judah were scattered among the nations after Babylon defeated them. So, we read in Ezek. 36:20, "they [i.e., the people of Judah] profaned my holy name, in that people said of them, 'These are the people of the LORD, and yet they had to go out of his land.'" You see, there was an element of truth in the nations' perception of Judah's plight. After all, God and Israel were bound together by a covenant. God was to be Israel's God and Israel was to be God's special, chosen people.

God's Promise to Hallow/Sanctify His Name

What should God do? He went on to speak of His plan:

> "But I had concern for *my holy name*, which the house of Israel had profaned among the nations to which they came.... It is not for your sake, O house of Israel, that I am about to act, but for My holy name, which you have profaned among the nations where you went. And I will vindicate the holiness of My great name which has been profaned among the nations, which you have profaned in their midst. Then the nations will know that I am the LORD... when I prove Myself holy among you in their sight" (Ezekiel 36:21-23).

Here we hear of God's concern for His holy name. But how would He vindicate His holy name—that is, how would He *hallow* His name? Should He just abandon His people? After all, His sinful people were the cause of His name being defiled! But He bound Himself to them by means of a solemn covenant with them and with their father, Abraham. If He were to abandon the covenant, His name would be profaned by His own action. And that, God can never do; He can never deny the sanctity and honor of His own name. Then, how could God hallow His name while remaining faithful to the covenant He made?

How God would Sanctify His Name

See what the Lord went on to say: "I will take you from the nations and gather you from all the countries and bring you into your own land" (Ezek. 36:24). As His name was profaned because the people of Israel were exiled from the land and scattered among the nations, He would hallow His name by restoring them to the land and blessing them in it.

But God did not stop there. What good would it be for His people to return to the Promised Land if they remained sinful? They would have to be cast out of the land again and the vicious cycle would continue (as it did in the time of the judges). So the Lord said,

> "I will sprinkle clean water on you, and you shall be clean from all your uncleannesses, and from all your idols I will cleanse you. And I will give you a new heart, and a new spirit I will put within you. And I will remove the heart of stone from your flesh and give you a heart of flesh. And I will put my Spirit within you, and cause you to walk in my statutes and be careful to obey my rules" (vv. 25-27).

When was this fulfilled? It was not fulfilled when the Jews returned from their exile in the sixth century, B.C. Even though they did physically return from the exile, the spiritual condition of the post-exilic Jews, as it is shown in the books of Ezra, Nehemiah, Malachi, etc., does not seem much improved from the days prior to the exile. Ezekiel's prophecy pointed to a later time when the sins of God's people would indeed be washed away fully and the Spirit of God poured out on them! When did this happen?

When the Promise was Fulfilled

We know the answer, don't we? Who can wash away our sins when they are too many to count, too horrible to recount? Who can pay for the eternal punishment we deserve for our rebellion against the infinitely holy God? Who can shield us from the wrath of God and satisfy His righteous anger against us? Who can heal our sin-sick souls and make us well again? Who can give us the new birth from heaven and create us anew? Who can grant us the Holy Spirit without destroying us in His all-consuming fire? Nothing but the blood of Jesus! Nothing but the atoning death of the true Lamb of God from heaven. Nothing but the perfect obedience of the eternal Son of God. Jesus alone can redeem us from the bondage of sin and death. Jesus alone can bear God's infinite wrath and turn away His righteous anger against us. Jesus alone can transform us, once objects of God's wrath, into God's own dear children. Jesus alone can baptize us with the Holy Spirit and give us a new birth from heaven.

Just because Jesus can doesn't mean He would or should. Yet He was willing to pay a costly price for our salvation, to suffer our misery, humiliation, suffering, and punishment, and to die the death we deserved. How amazing! When God decided to enter into a covenant with sinners and save them from their sins, He knew what that would entail. He knew that His honor would be subjected to humiliation and His holy name would be defiled on account of His sinful people—all because He bound Himself to them by a covenant. But the humiliation, which Israel brought upon the Lord by its defeat and exile, was nothing compared to the humiliation He would have to endure for the eternal salvation of His people—"He himself bore our sins in his body on the tree, that we might die to sin and live to righteousness" (1 Pet. 2:24).

This was exactly what He had in mind when God walked through the path of self-malediction between the cut-up pieces of animals, which Abraham arranged at His command (Gen. 15). When others performed this ceremony, it was to say, "I will keep the covenant because I don't want to be cursed as these animals!" But when God did it, it was to say, "I must, and I will, undergo this curse because this is the only way to save My sinful people and bless them!" Amazingly, God was fully prepared to do this when He entered into covenant with His people and bound His glory to the fate of His people. And He did it when His Son came into this world and bore the curse of our sin.

But His death was not the end of the story. He who was crucified and buried was raised from the dead on the third day and ascended to heaven and was seated at the right hand of God. God thus exalted His faithful and obedient Son above every name that every knee should bow and every tongue confess that Jesus Christ is Lord to the glory of His Father. God exalted Jesus because He accomplished His messianic mission to save His people from their sins once for all. Finally, God vindicated (or, hallowed) His name by saving His people unto eternal life—what He promised to do in Ezekiel and all throughout the Old Testament.

How Jesus is the Answer to This Petition

So then, what are we praying for when we pray, "Hallowed be Thy name"? In essence, we are praying for Jesus Christ, our Redeemer, aren't we? In view of God's covenant with His people, there was no way for God's holy name to be hallowed apart from saving His people from sin. If so, *in praying for the hallowing*

41

of God's name, we are praying for Jesus to suffer and die for our salvation. Oh, to think that it was Jesus who taught His disciples to pray this petition! I wonder what went through Jesus' mind as He taught this prayer.

So, we find a very important feature of the Lord's Prayer that we shall affirm again and again in this series: *if this prayer is called the Lord's Prayer, it is not only because the Lord Himself taught it but also because the ultimate answer to its petitions is the Lord Jesus Christ Himself.* Should we be surprised? After all, what can be the greatest desire of God's people? What can be the greatest reward for us? Can it be other than Jesus Christ? Can there be anything better than to have the Lord as our reward and inheritance?

How This Petition Affects Us

This petition presupposes and looks forward to our salvation in Jesus Christ. After all, how can insolent sinners like us desire the hallowing of God's name when we are the ones who defiled His name in the first place? This is possible only when we are born again, born from above by the Spirit of Christ. And as we pray this petition, we are praying that our hearts be conformed more and more to Jesus Christ, who willingly laid down His life for the hallowing of His Father's name, so that the glory of God's holy name becomes the greatest desire of our hearts more and more. As we abandon ourselves and seek first the hallowing of God's name, we become, in a wonderful way, the very answer to this prayer in Jesus Christ. For God's holy name is hallowed as we are redeemed, as we are sanctified more and more in the likeness of Jesus Christ. Oh, how our lives are so wonderfully hidden with Christ in God!

As you may have noticed already, this petition has been answered "already and not yet." It has been answered already in that we have been baptized by the Holy Spirit and all our sins are forgiven once for all in our justification by faith (1 Cor. 12:13). But it has not been answered yet because we are not perfectly walking in God's statutes and obeying His rules (Ezek. 36:27). He is working in us to bring it about in our sanctification, which will come to its glorious consummation at His Second Coming.

This, only our Lord Jesus can do. And He will do it as surely as He came because He is faithful. He will save us wholly and completely. God who justified us in Jesus Christ will sanctify us and glorify us. The zeal of the Lord will do this (Isa. 9:7). For He is most zealous for the honor of His holy name. And He will never fail. Oh, praise God that our salvation is bound up with the hallowing of God's name! That alone is our hope! As His name was sanctified and glorified through the life, death, and resurrection of Jesus Christ, so it will be to the fullest measure when Christ shall return to bring to completion His wonderful work of redemption. Let us, then, live with confidence in God's unfailing faithfulness to His covenant promise! And let our deepest longing be for Jesus Christ our Lord and Savior! And may the Lord hallow His name by sanctifying us more and more from glory to glory, grace upon grace!

"Your Kingdom Come"
(Jesus, the King)

The second petition is, "Your kingdom come."

"Your *kingdom* come"
A Kingdom or a Democratic Nation?

Let us notice first, that, it is for a *kingdom* that we are praying. A kingdom! To pray for a kingdom in this 21st century may seem hopelessly outdated and absurd. Just take a look at the kingdoms that are still in existence. Most of them are monarchies in name only. Kings and queens have become symbolic figures without any real political, military power. Kingdoms and royalty are on the way out, only to exist in the worn-out pages of bygone history or the colorful pages of tabloids. So, we must keep in mind that the kind of kingdom we are praying for in this petition is a kingdom in its proper sense, the kind of kingdom that Jesus' original audience had in mind—a state in which a king is its sovereign ruler. When we place our trust in Jesus Christ, we are brought into a kingdom, not into a democratic republic.

Living in a democratic republic, we don't know what it is like to live under a king's sovereign rule. Something that comes closest to it has got to be the military life. We have a friend, who is a Marine. He is now deployed in the Middle East. This is his fourth deployment in four years. He is married and this is taking a toll on his marriage, as we can imagine. Just when they are about to get adjusted and begin to get settled down in their relationship, he is called out again on another deployment. When he is called upon like that by the military, he has no choice. It doesn't matter that he is in the middle of marriage counseling, which is just beginning to turn things around in the way he and his wife relate to each other. He has got to go whenever and wherever the military sends him. No ifs, ands, or buts. That is the kind of authority king has in a kingdom. Do we realize what we are doing when we pray, "Your kingdom come..."? Who would want to pray such a thing?

The idea of kingdom is offensive to our sensibility. We are a fiercely independent people. Think of how we came into being as a nation. It does not sit well with us that anyone should have any authority or control over us, much less a royal, imperial rule. What is more, we have all heard the saying, "Absolute power corrupts absolutely." So, we cherish and take pride in our democratic form of government. We try to promote it throughout the world.

Limitations of Democracy

But democracy is not without its problems. Obviously, a system, which is governed by its citizens, rises and falls by the quality of the citizens—how good, wise, well-informed, and courageous they are. But the general populace usually lacks the time and the expertise that are needed to make wise decisions on important and complex matters of the state—especially in a nation like ours, which is vastly bigger and more complicated than the ancient Greek city states. We all need to be better educated and informed as we participate in the democratic process. But who of us has the time to keep tabs on what is going on in all the branches of the government—executive, legislative, and judicial—and at all the levels of the government—federal, state, and local?

So, we elect our representatives to work on our behalf. But think about all the decisions that are made every day at all these different branches and levels of our government. Many of them have huge implications for our daily life and, some of them, for many generations to come. We cannot even keep up with the news about the most controversial ones! How can we keep track of all of them? Do we know our representatives well enough to trust them to do the right thing? We are not surprised that Plato's preference was monarchy governed by a virtuous philosopher king—that is, if such a person exists and if he can be induced to leave the ivory tower to get involved in the messy business of politics without being corrupted by the political process and the power given to him.

But I very much doubt that any of us would like to adopt monarchy as our form of government. Why? Our nation as a democratic republic adores the notion of determining our own path and creating our own destiny. We may fail in the end but we prize the right to say, "At least I did it my way!" This is why most of us *feel* safer to drive. Why? Because *we* are in control (regardless of our driving skills). It is hard to imagine modern nations going back to monarchy. Besides, who is reliable enough for our absolute confidence—virtuous and wise and competent enough to earn our absolute and unconditional trust?

The Real Problem with Political Systems

The problem is not with the form of government. The problem is, rather, the absence of the kind of rulers who are virtuous and competent enough to be entrusted with the authority and power to govern us. This problem does not just exist in monarchy. We face the same problem (in a smaller measure, perhaps) whenever the election season rolls around. Fresh faces and catchy slogans and ubiquitous political ads wake us up from our slumber of apathy and distrust. We listen to them and follow their campaigns, thinking and hoping that maybe the particular candidate of our choice is an exception. But deep inside we cannot shake off that nagging suspicion that their bark of promise is louder than their bite of execution. And their proposed solutions, while they sound good, may have unintended and unforeseen consequences, doing more harm than good. Our problems are too big and complex for anyone to solve. Our political system might have been compromised. And politicians are... politicians.

And yet, we participate in the election process out of our civic duty and we choose our candidates, hoping against hope, perhaps. Even so, we manage to get pretty emotional about it. Arguments break out among strangers, friendships get strained, and family members don't talk to one another. Why—when we all know that these politicians will disappoint us in one way or the other? Are we just foolish? Do we all suffer from "election amnesia"?

But we must be careful not to see a speck in the politicians' eyes while we neglect the log in our own eyes. The failures of the politicians are magnified because they are public figures. How about us with our own individual, private problems? Are we wiser and more virtuous than they? Do we know what to do when we find ourselves in moral dilemmas? When we are confronted with what we *ought* to do and what we *want* to do, do we have the moral courage to do what is right instead of what feels good?

So, we have come full circle, haven't we? When we are young, we may be able to get away with saying, "I believe in myself." But a person of enough life experience and self-reflection would say, "I can't trust myself!" Our problem in the end is not the environment or the form of government. Our biggest problem is ourselves. If everyone were virtuous, even a bad political system would work just fine! What, then, is the solution? Wherein lies our hope?

How about "Your kingdom come"?

Is it so crazy to pray, "*Your* kingdom come"? What would it be like to have a king, who is impeccably virtuous and absolutely incorruptible in His character, wholeheartedly devoted to the good of His people, wise beyond measure, and almighty in His power? That is precisely what we have in the kingdom of God, isn't it? If so, what is more natural and more urgent than to pray that God's kingdom come?

There is nothing humiliating about giving people the respect they deserve. There is no shame in following wise advice, obeying a good rule, submitting to a legitimate authority, admiring a work of excellence, and accepting the truth. It is foolish to insist on our own ideas simply because they are ours, for no other reason than the fact that they came out of our brain. But that is precisely what we do in sinful pride. We all know the powerful grip of sin, which makes us do what is obviously so foolish and self-destructive.

Submitting to God's sovereign rule is the safest and wisest thing to do. Who is wiser than God? Who is more powerful than God?

Whose mind is big enough to grasp the "big picture" AND pay attention to the smallest details except God's omniscient mind? Who is good except God alone (Mark 10:18)? Who cares about justice and righteousness more than God? "Righteousness and justice are the foundation of [His] throne; steadfast love and faithfulness go before [Him]" (Ps. 89:14). And who loves and cares for us more than God? He did not spare His own Son but gave Him up for us all (Gal. 2:2). Will He not also with Him graciously give us all things (Rom. 8:32)?

"*Your* kingdom come"
A Kingdom Greater than David's

At this point, it may sound redundant to say that the kingdom we are praying for is the kingdom *of God*—"*Your* kingdom come." But we must appreciate its significance in its historical context.

When the Jews of that time heard this petition, what do you think came to their minds? Very likely, it was the restoration of the Davidic monarchy. They were under Roman occupation. And the one who sat on the throne of their land was Herod the Idumean, who was certainly no son of David! Oh, how the Jews must have longed to be rid of the Romans and have David's offspring sit on the throne in Jerusalem!

This longing was reflected in the chants with which the crowd welcomed Jesus into Jerusalem: "Hosanna! Blessed is he who comes in the name of the Lord! Blessed is the *coming kingdom of our father David!* Hosanna in the highest" (Mark 11:9-10)! This was also what preoccupied the disciples' minds even at the moment of Jesus' ascension. Their final question to Jesus was, "Lord, will you at this time *restore* the kingdom to Israel" (Acts 1:6)? Obviously, something that needs to be restored had to exist before.

There was a sense in which the kingdom of David (that is, the nation of Israel) was the kingdom of God. For God was the ultimate King of Israel. Israel's human kings had to rule according to the law He gave at Mount Sinai (Deut. 17:18-20). This included David. As king, David was to shepherd the people of Israel. But he did not forget that, at the end of the day, even he was but a sheep and the Lord was his Shepherd (Ps. 23:1), the true King of Israel. The kingdom of Israel was not David's; it was ultimately God's.

With the words of this petition, Jesus shows that the kingdom of God is much more than the kingdom of David. When Jesus speaks of God's kingdom here ("Your kingdom"), we know that He is referring specifically to "the kingdom of heaven." The kingdom of heaven has been a central thrust of His message from the beginning of His public ministry (Matt. 3:2), a central theme of His teaching and parables. The kingdom of heaven is certainly a central theme in the Sermon on the Mount, in which the Lord's Prayer is found. By referring to the kingdom of God as the kingdom of heaven, Jesus was making a clear distinction between the *heavenly* kingdom of God and the *earthly* kingdom of David/Israel. In this petition, Jesus is teaching us to pray for *God's heavenly* kingdom to be established on earth.

"Your kingdom *come*"
A Stone Cut out by no Human Hand

Notice also that Jesus is teaching us to pray for the *coming* of God's kingdom. If what we are praying for is God's *heavenly* kingdom, then this kingdom must come to us from heaven; it is not something we can build with our efforts. This idea of God's kingdom "coming" is most dramatically described in Dan. 2. There we have an account of Nebuchadnezzar's disturbing dream and Daniel's explanation of it. The dream consisted of a statue and a stone. The statue was awesome in its appearance. It was made of gold, silver, bronze, iron and clay, making up different parts of the statue. This statue represented the kingdoms of the world. It was a statue of man because it represented the city of man. It was a kingdom *of* man, *for* man, and *by* man. It was all about the glory of man.

The vision also had in it a stone. This stone "was cut out by no human hands..., struck the image on its feet of iron and clay, and broke them in pieces" (Dan. 2:34). No description is given of this stone except that it was "cut out by no human hands." We know why. Contrary to the statue in the shape of a man, which represented the glory of human accomplishments, this stone was cut out without human hands. God Himself would set up this kingdom with no (meritorious) help of man. This stone, according to Daniel's interpretation, represented God's kingdom: "And in the days of those kings the God of heaven will set up a kingdom which will never be destroyed..." (2:44). The stone came out of a mountain (2:45), and mountains were considered the dwelling places of the gods. The stone destroyed the statue and grew miraculously and supernaturally into a great mountain and filled the whole earth.

The second petition prays for what this stone represents: the eternal kingdom of God. The kingdom of God must *come* because man cannot build it with his own hands, which are tainted with sin and blood. The kingdom of God must *come* because it is not of this world. It must come from God; it must come from heaven. It transcends, and must transcend, the kingdom of Israel. It transcends, and must transcend, even God's first creation, which was subject to corruption and defilement. So it is most appropriately called the kingdom of *heaven*.

Only God Can Bring His Kingdom

No one can bring this kingdom except God Himself. That is why Jesus taught His disciples to *pray* for God's kingdom to come. What is prayer? It is an expression of the total helplessness of those who pray. Think of the typical gestures and postures of prayer: clasped hands, arms opened wide and eyes lifted up toward heaven, bended knees, the whole body prostrated on the ground, etc. These postures express total humility and complete surrender. He who prays must bend his stiff neck and bow his proud head in total submission to God. He who enters the sanctuary of prayer must take off his sandals of self-reliance and cross the threshold of self-surrender. There is no room for pride in prayer. There is no place for self-sufficiency or self-reliance in prayer. This is even more so when we pray for the coming of God's kingdom.

When we pray *this* prayer, as Jesus has taught us, we don't have to wonder whether our longing will be realized. There is absolutely no possibility that this petition will not come to its glorious fruition. For God is already the King of all kings and Lord of all lords. In this petition, we are not asking the kingdom to come into existence. Nor are we praying it because the kingdom of God is not here. Since God created the world, it is *His* kingdom. The Psalmists sing repeatedly, "The Lord reigns!" What we are praying for in this petition is for the kingdom of God to be here in a particular mode—"as it is in heaven" where there is no gap between God's revealed will (i.e., His law) and the actual state of affairs.

The Answer—the (First) Coming of Jesus

In fact, this petition was being answered even as Jesus was teaching this prayer. For He is the King of heaven, who came into this world. Since there cannot be a kingdom without a king, we cannot expect the kingdom of heaven to come without the coming of heaven's King. But if the King of heaven comes, we can be sure that the kingdom of heaven comes with Him. He is a living stone, cut out of the heavenly mountain of God with no human hand. By Himself without the help of any man, He overcame sin and hell and Satan and the world. Yet, the kingdom of God grows into a great mountain that fills the whole earth as the gospel is proclaimed throughout the world.

But how was He to usher in the kingdom of heaven? What would happen to this world when the kingdom of heaven should come? In praying this petition, we are not praying for the *eradication* of this creation. Rather, we are praying for the *redemption* of this creation along with God's people (Rom. 8:19-23). Crucial, then, is addressing the problem of sin: sin must be punished, its power and influence done away with, and its presence removed.

In order to fulfill this petition, the King of heaven came in humility as the Suffering Servant of the Lord—to the shock of the Jews, becoming a stumbling block to them. Why? Why couldn't He rule over His kingdom from His exalted throne in heaven, seated between the wings of the cherubim, as He did in the Old Testament? Why couldn't He simply command from heaven that sin be removed, sinners be punished, and His people be redeemed? Why did He have to come as the Suffering Servant of the Lord?

Because our salvation cannot be accomplished with swords or spears, with guns and tanks. Our salvation is from sin. We need pardon for our sins. We need to meet the standard of righteousness for the people of God. We can do neither on our own. We need God's grace to save us. The problem is that God is also just. In extending His grace to us, He cannot ignore His justice. He cannot deny Himself in any way and still be God. So, God's saving grace cannot be an arbitrary act of God's divine prerogative: He cannot forgive His people just because He wants to and He is God. Such a pardon may be gracious but it is not just. God's saving grace must be a *righteous* grace—a grace which not only meets our desperate need for God's grace but also satisfies God's justice.

His Voluntary Humiliation

This is why the Son of God had to come in the weakness of our body as the Suffering Servant of the Lord. Paul says, "…though he was in the form of God, [Jesus Christ] did not count equality with God a thing to be grasped, but emptied himself, by taking the form of a servant, being born in the likeness of men. And being found in human form, he humbled himself by becoming obedient to the point of death, even death on a cross" (Phil. 2:6-8). Why did He have to humble Himself so much? It is because we in our sinful pride rejected God's sovereign authority over us. We exalted ourselves as the masters of our own destinies as if we were gods. So, the Son of God humbled Himself and subjected Himself to the humiliation of incarnation and became like us.

He did so in order to suffer and die in our place to pay the penalty of our sins. This was *gracious* because Someone else was punished in our place so we might freely receive God's forgiveness. It also satisfied God's *justice* because the due penalty of sin was paid, fully and completely. His resurrection testifies to the full payment of sin. He could not be brought back to life as long as the penalty of sin, which is death, remained. Therefore, those who put their trust in Jesus Christ do not come into judgment but have passed out of death to life (John 5:24). "He has delivered us from the domain of darkness and transferred us to the kingdom of his beloved Son…" (Col. 1:13). This kingdom, which is free from the power of sin and death and Satan, is eternal and incorruptible. And this kingdom, which was inaugurated by the death and resurrection of Jesus Christ, will be consummated in glory and beauty when the King returns as the Judge of the living and the dead!

Until He Returns

What are we to do in the meantime, as we pray for the glorious fulfillment of this petition? Our Short Catechism says,

> "In the second petition (which is, Thy kingdom come) we pray, that Satan's kingdom may be destroyed; and that the kingdom of grace may be advanced, ourselves and others brought into it, and kept in it; and that the kingdom of glory may be hastened" (A. 102).

This petition will be fully answered by God's divine intervention at the end of history. But God is at work even now, advancing His kingdom throughout this world. Think about what is happening in China, India, and even in the Middle East, as more and more people are professing their faith in Jesus Christ despite the persecution that awaits them. The kingdom of heaven no longer manifests itself through a particular nation as in the Old Testament. It is now through the church of Jesus Christ and the witness of God's people, who live for the glory of God in joyful obedience to their gracious King in every aspect of their lives, in whose lives the grip of sin is loosened more and more as they make their every word, deed, and thought captive to the obedience of Christ (2 Cor. 10:5). Let us consider it our greatest joy and privilege to have God as our King. Oh, what safety, what promise of victory and abundant provision, what joy inexpressible is ours in our wonderful King!

"Your Will be Done"
(Jesus, the Fulfillment of God's Will)

"Your will be done"
"Your-Petitions"

The third petition of the Lord's Prayer is, "Your will be done, on earth as it is in heaven." This is the last of the first three petitions, which are called "Your-petitions" for obvious reasons: "Hallowed be *Your* name. *Your* kingdom come. *Your* will be done on earth as it is in heaven." But these petitions do not just share the word "Your." They also have the same word order. If we translate the Greek, preserving the word order, these petitions would read like this: "Hallowed be Your name. Come Your kingdom. Be done Your will, as in heaven also on earth." In each petition, the verb comes first, then the subject, which has the word "Your." But the third petition is unique. It has an extra phrase attached to it: "on earth as it is in heaven."

There seems to be somewhat of a progression, or direction, in these "Your-petitions." The first petition, "Hallowed be Your name," does not have a verb like "come" or an expression like "on earth as it is in heaven," which indicates a movement in a downward direction. It is only implied that God's holy name will be hallowed in the realm of creation. But in the second petition, "Your kingdom come," there is a definite movement. The kingdom of God is *coming*. It doesn't say where it is coming from (this is implied but not specified) but it is coming to where we are. What is only implied in the second is made clear in the third petition, "Your will be done on earth as it is in heaven." In this petition, the direction of the movement is clearly spelled out: the direction is from heaven to earth. And there is a sense of finality: God's will shall finally be done "on earth as it is in heaven."

The Movement of the "Your-Petitions"

These "Your-petitions" are joined together not only by the fact that they all contain "Your" and by their word order, but also by this directional progression. It is very likely that what is clearly spelled out in the third petition applies to the first two as well. We are asking that God's name be hallowed on earth as it is in heaven, that His kingdom come to earth from heaven, and that His will be done on earth as it is in heaven. What these petitions request is none other than the intrusion of heaven, which is the proper abode of God, into this world, which is the realm of man.

What is more, the third petition marks the major transition in the Lord's Prayer: as it ends the "Your-petitions," it anticipates the "Us-petitions." It does so by spelling out the movement *from heaven to earth*—"Your will be done, *on earth as it is in heaven*." As we will see, the "Us-petitions" show the earthly effects, or benefits, of this heavenly intrusion into the world.

This "heaven-to-earth" direction of the Lord's Prayer doesn't mean that this world is what is ultimate and final. When the kingdom of God comes into this world, it is not altered and consumed by the world; it overcomes and conquers. Earth is temporary. Heaven is eternal. The kingdom of God/heaven will be the last kingdom standing, not the kingdoms of this world. Such is the idea that the third petition expresses clearly: "Your will be done *on earth as it is in heaven.*" God's will shall be done on earth *as it is in heaven.* The Lord's Prayer as a whole declares the supremacy of the divine over the human, the heavenly over the earthly, the eternal over the temporal, the eschatological over the present. ("Eschatological" in theology means that which pertains to the age to come, which is eternal and heavenly.)

A Logical Prayer

So, Jesus teaches His disciples to pray, "Your will be done on earth as it is in heaven." In praying to God, there can be nothing more logical than to say, "Your will be done." After all, God is the sovereign King of heaven and earth. It is His world, not ours. It is He who owns all things by virtue of His creation. We are His creatures, though privileged to bear His image. We are but tenants in His world, His subjects in His kingdom.

If so, should we counsel God and tell the sovereign King what to do and what not to do, even in our petitions? Should we ever say, "My will be done" instead of "Your will be done"? How good is our will, our desire? At times we don't even know what we really want. In so many instances, the only thing we are sure about is what we *don't* want. We want what is good but we often don't have a clear idea as to what that may be. Why is our decision making so difficult? We don't know which decision will lead to good because our analysis of the past is inaccurate, our assessment of the present is incomplete, and our vision of the future is near-sighted. As such finite, limited creatures, do we dare to advise the God of infinite wisdom and knowledge?

We can characterize our mind as primarily "logical" in nature—we move linearly from one idea to another, adding to our knowledge one thing after another. God's mind, on the other hand, can be characterized as "intuitive"—He knows all things all at once, each of them individually as well as everything in its connection with everything else. Infinite in His wisdom and knowledge, He declares the end from the beginning (Isa. 46:10); He has foreordained all things according to the counsel of His will (Eph. 1:11). "Where is the wise man? Where is the scribe? Where is the debater of this age...? [T]he foolishness of God is wiser than men, and the weakness of God is stronger than men" (1 Cor. 1:20, 25).

What is more, God is infinitely good and gracious toward His people. That is why we should never insist on our own will over God's, which stems from His infinite wisdom and goodness. God's will cannot be improved upon because what He wills stems out of His perfection. What God has willed from the foundation of the world is unchangeable and eternal because it is insuperably best—best, that is, for achieving His purpose, not merely for our convenience. God cannot will what is second best. And He loves us too much to change His will for ours. In fact, when the Bible uses the language of God giving in to someone's will, it does as a curse: "God gave them up in the lusts of their hearts to impurity, to the dishonoring of their bodies among themselves, because they exchanged the truth about God for a lie and worshiped and served the creature rather than the Creator, who is blessed forever" (Rom. 1:24-25)! C.S. Lewis said, "There are two kinds of people: those who say to God, 'Thy will be done,' and those to whom God says, in the end, 'Thy will be done.' All that are in Hell, choose it."[5]

---

5 C.S. Lewis, *The Great Divorce* (HarperOne, 2001), p. 75.

It is not just our creaturely limitations our will suffers from; it suffers also from our fallen condition. Take our selfishness, for instance. Our selfishness would not be a big problem if we were wise enough to know and good enough to desire what is truly good for us. But often, that is not the case. In fact, a fallen sinner in his unregenerate state never wants what is truly good for him/her. I'm sure all of us can look back on our lives and think of certain things that we wanted so much at that time but are relieved that God did not grant them to us.

"Your will be done" in Greco-Roman Religions
So, Lohmeyer asks rhetorically, "[I]f religion is reverence and submission to the will of God or the gods, should it not be possible to find similar echoes [of the third petition] in all religions"?[6] Then he goes on to affirm it, saying, "There is, for example, in Greek and Roman religion the kindred formula 'If God wills', or 'According to the will of the gods'…. [W]hen [Pythagorean Thymaridas] was parting from friends to go on a sea journey, one of them called to him, 'May the gods grant you what you will.' He retorted, 'God forbid, I would wish to be granted what the gods will.'"[7]

Its Absence in the Old Testament

Then he goes on to say something that is quite shocking: "[B]ut there is hardly any evidence of it in the Old Testament."[8] How can this be? If anything, the Old Testament is about God's sovereignty. Shouldn't we expect the Old Testament to be replete with many prayers of "Your will be done"? Lohmeyer offers an explanation as to why that is not the case: "For there [in the Old

6 Earnst Lohmeyer, *"Our Fahter": An Introduction to the Lord's Prayer*, Harper & Row: New York, 1965), p. 115.
7 *Ibid.*
8 *Ibid.*

Testament] the will of God is not to be discerned gradually in the events of human life; it is revealed in the Law as the norm of all life and conduct; it is therefore not so much a matter of *willing* what God wills, but of *doing* what God wills...."[9]

How This Petition Differs from the Greco-Roman Prayers

Then, is the third petition Jesus' adaptation of the Greco-Roman religious sentiment, departing from the theology of the Old Testament Judaism? Certainly not. Consider the reasons behind the two different approaches to the will of the divine. We can say that the Greco-Roman approach is a fatalistic surrender to the divine will. There are two key features to this: one is the *irresistibility* of the divine will; the other is man's *ignorance* of the divine will. So then, a religious man is someone who surrenders himself to the outworking of the divine will. This is not necessarily done out of a deep sense of trust but rather out of fear. The gods of the Greek and Roman mythologies do not exactly command trust for their goodness. But they do command fear for their power and jealousy.

In fact, the Greco-Roman mythologies are replete with instances of tragic ends for those who tried to defy divine will. People did not know what their powerful yet capricious gods would do to them, especially if they got angry at them or jealous of them. But they knew enough not to challenge their will. The only sane option for them was to surrender themselves to whatever these gods willed. That way, at least, they would not suffer additional disasters that were sure to come if they defied the will of the gods!

The Jews and God's Revealed Will

The Jews must have known that God's revealed will was not all there was to God's will. Moses told them, "The secret things

---

9 Lohmeyer, p. 116.

belong to the LORD our God, but the things that are revealed belong to us and to our children forever, that we may do all the words of this law" (Deut. 29:29). They knew not to inquire into God's secret will.[10] Their accountability was to God's revealed will—namely, to God's Law—not to God's secret will. That is why their emphasis was *doing* the will of God, which was clearly revealed to them in the Law.

But what did the history of Israel demonstrate? The Israelites utterly failed to do God's will even though it was clearly revealed to them. That was why they were driven out of the Promised Land as the Canaanites before them. Even though they were able to return and rebuild the temple after the Babylonian Captivity, life was never the same. Other than a brief period of independence during the Maccabean era, Israel could not fully regain its independence from foreign powers. Even at the time of Jesus, Israel was under Roman occupation. All this had a lot to do Israel's failure to do the will of God. So, throughout the Gospels we see the wickedness of the religious leaders and the people of Israel lost like sheep without a shepherd (Matt. 9:36). Even the temple, which was the religious center of Israel, was so commercialized that Jesus had to drive out all the merchants, crying out, "It is written, 'My house shall be called a house of prayer,' but you make it a den of robbers" (Matt. 21:13)!

It is important to consider the deplorable spiritual condition of Israel at that time—their failure to do the will of God as it was revealed in the Law—as the context in which our Lord gives this third petition. "Your will" in this petition is referring not so

---

10 God's secret will allows even things that seem contradictory to His revealed will. This is why it would be disastrous to make God's secret will the standard of our actions. We would be able to justify all our sins since God's secret will allowed them. But God will judge according to His revealed will, not according to His secret will, which we do not know anyway.

much to God's *secret* will (as was the focus of the Greco-Roman religiosity) as to God's *revealed* will in the Law. If that is the case, what does it mean to pray that God's (revealed) will be done? The law was given for *His people* to do, not for *God* to do, was it? And after all these years, after their repeated failures to keep God's law, were they to pray that they would somehow do God's (revealed) will now? What is this petition asking God to do?

God's Promise to Do His Will

Actually, it is something that God had already promised to do. We read in Jer. 31:31-34,

> "Behold, the days are coming, declares the LORD, when I will make a new covenant with the house of Israel and the house of Judah, not like the covenant that I made with their fathers on the day when I took them by the hand to bring them out of the land of Egypt, my covenant that they broke, though I was their husband, declares the LORD. For this is the covenant that I will make with the house of Israel after those days, declares the LORD: I will put my law within them, and I will write it on their hearts. And I will be their God, and they shall be my people. And no longer shall each one teach his neighbor and each his brother, saying, 'Know the LORD,' for they shall all know me, from the least of them to the greatest, declares the LORD. For I will forgive their iniquity, and I will remember their sin no more."

Here we see how God's (revealed) will was to be done: God would put His law within His people, writing it on their hearts rather than on the tablets of stone. This was another way of saying that they would be able to actually keep the law rather than just know it and break it. This is precisely what would differentiate this new covenant from the old covenant, which is characterize as "my covenant that they broke." Ezekiel expressed it in this way:

"I will sprinkle clean water on you, and you shall be clean from all your uncleannesses, and from all your idols I will cleanse you. I will give you a new heart, and a new spirit I will put within you. And I will remove the heart of stone from your flesh and give you a heart of flesh. And I will put my Spirit within you, and cause you to walk in my statutes and be careful to obey my rules" (Ezek. 36:26-27).

God's people would finally be able to keep God's law and it would be made possible through God's endowment of the Holy Spirit on their hearts!

God's Will and the New Covenant in Jesus

We can say, then, that the third petition, "Your will be done…," is a prayer that God would establish this new covenant. Again, we see that the answer to this prayer is found in Jesus Christ, who is the Mediator of the new covenant. We are familiar with the words, with which our Lord established the Lord's Supper, specifically in the distribution of wine: "This cup that is poured out for you is *the new covenant* in my blood" (Luke 22:20); "This cup is *the new covenant* in my blood. Do this, as often as you drink it, in remembrance of me" (1 Cor. 11:25). Jesus spoke of His blood particularly in relation to the new covenant because blood was what was used to ratify a covenant in the Ancient Near Eastern culture.

Jesus' words were designed to remind the disciples of Moses' words, which he used to ratify Israel's covenant with God at

Mount Sinai: "Behold *the blood of the covenant* that the LORD has made with you in accordance with all these words" (Ex. 24:8). Moses was speaking of the blood of *young bulls* (NASB), which were sacrificed for this covenant-making ceremony. Jesus spoke of *His own blood*, which was about to be poured out to establish the new covenant. Obviously, He was highlighting the contrast between the old covenant, which was made with the blood of bulls, and the new covenant, which was being made with His own blood.

The Breakable Old Covenant and the Unbreakable New Covenant

This contrast explains why the old covenant was breakable and broken while the new covenant is unbreakable and eternal. The old covenant was ratified by the blood of bulls after the law was read and Israel made a vow, saying, "All the words that the LORD has spoken we will do" (Ex. 24:3). But Israel failed to keep the law. Not only that, Israel rejected God's appointed Messiah, Jesus, when they chose Barabbas, a notorious criminal, over Jesus. And they rejected God as their King when they said to Pontius Pilate, "We have no king but Caesar" (John 19:15)!

The new covenant, on the other hand, is ratified by the blood of Jesus Christ. This new covenant is unbreakable because the blood of Jesus Christ was shed to pay the penalty of our sins once for all, "not in part but the whole"! Sin, as it is disobedience and rebellion against God, is the only thing that can break man's covenant with God. But God nailed all our sins to the cross in the crucifixion of Jesus Christ. The new covenant ratified by His sin-forgiving, guilt-erasing, shame-removing blood cannot be broken. God's promise to forgive the iniquity of His people and to remember their sins no more (Jer. 31:34) is finally fulfilled in the sacrificial death of Jesus Christ!

The New Covenant and the Holy Spirit

Jesus also spoke of our need to be born of *water* and *the Spirit* (John 3:5). When Jesus said this to Nicodemus, He was speaking of what Ezekiel prophesied of—how God would sprinkle clean *water* on His people to cleanse them (Ezek. 36:25) and put *His Spirit* within them to cause them to walk in His statutes (Ezek. 36:27). For this to happen, however, Jesus had to be lifted up as Moses lifted up the bronze serpent in the wilderness (John 3:14). Of course, this referred to His death on the cross. As the Jews were healed of the venomous bite of the vipers by beholding the bronze serpent on a wooden pole, so will everyone be saved from the hell-inducing bite of sin if he puts his faith in the Son of God lifted on the wooden, rugged cross.

The penalty-paying death of Jesus Christ also enabled God's people to receive the Holy Spirit. Unforgiven sinners cannot hope to receive the Holy Spirit. For He is a consuming fire, who engulfs in His holy wrath all that is sinful. John the Baptist spoke of Jesus' Holy Spirit baptism in this way: "He will baptize you with the Holy Spirit and fire. His winnowing fork is in his hand, and he will clear his threshing floor and gather his wheat into the barn, but the chaff he will burn with unquenchable fire" (Matt. 3:11-12). The Holy Spirit is an unquenchable fire, with which Jesus will burn all the unrepentant sinners like chaff. (The lake of fire in hell is none other than the Holy Spirit manifesting Himself as a consuming fire.) How can this Unquenchable Fire be a blessing to some, to those who believe in Jesus' name? Because Jesus paid the penalty of their sins by enduring the unquenchable fire of hell in their place. This induced Him to cry out as He was dying on the cross, "I thirst!"[11] Because of Jesus, the Consuming

---

11 Of all the painful things He could have spoken of during His crucifixion, why did Jesus only mention His thirst? It was because His thirst was caused by the fiery sword of God's judgment and, as such, was infinitely more painful than all the physical agony He experienced on the cross.

Fire that torments unrepentant sinners in hell is the Fire that cleanses, refines, and sanctifies those who are in Christ Jesus and gives them warmth, light, and life.

"On earth as it is in heaven"
God's Will in Heaven and on Earth

We can also see how God's will was done on earth as it is in heaven in Jesus Christ. Heaven is where God's revealed will is carried out perfectly without any exception or violation. Earth, on the other hand, has been a place where God's revealed will is constantly violated ever since the Fall: "The LORD saw that the wickedness of man was great in the earth, and that every intention of the thoughts of his heart was only evil continually" (Gen. 6:5). This doesn't apply only to Noah's generation: "For all have sinned and fall short of the glory of God" (Rom. 3:23); "None is righteous, no, not one" (Rom. 3:10). Both in sins of commission and omission, and in thought, word, and deed, we are all guilty of breaking God's law. Only Jesus Christ fulfilled God's will on earth as it is in heaven: "we do not have a high priest who is unable to sympathize with our weaknesses, but one who in every respect has been tempted as we are, yet without sin" (Heb. 4:15).

Jesus' Obedience to God's Will
Jesus' life of obedience reached its climax at the Garden of Gethsemane where He prayed, not just once but three times, "Father, if you are willing, remove this cup from me. Nevertheless, *not my will, but yours, be done*" (Luke 22:42). This was it, the most critical moment in all of redemptive history. Whether God's will would be done or not depended on what Jesus would do at this moment. Would He run from the cup of wrath or would He drink it to the dregs?

There is a sense that every moment of Jesus life up to this point was a critical moment in redemptive history. If Jesus sinned at any moment in His life, God's redemptive plan would have collapsed in failure and the whole humanity would have been condemned to hell forever. For a guilty sinner cannot die for others. But the moment of reckoning had finally arrived. After Peter's confession that Jesus was the Christ, the Son of the living God, Jesus started to speak of His coming suffering, death, and resurrection (Matt. 16:16). The Gospels don't tell us what Jesus was feeling at that time. There is no doubt that His feelings of sorrow were deep and powerful. But Jesus in the Garden of Gethsemane was only hours away from the cross. The moment of reckoning being so close, Jesus struggled enough to wonder whether there was another way to achieve man's salvation, to actually ask the Father to remove the cup of wrath from Him, and to pray this same prayer not just once but three times in the course of that one fateful night.

The gravity of this moment was comparable to what happened at the beginning of history in another garden, in which the First Adam was tempted by the evil one. Adam's failure at that crucial moment brought misery and death to the world, which was originally made "very good." But where the First Adam failed, the Second Adam succeeded. Despite His monumental struggle, Jesus chose to follow God's will, not His own. He chose to obey God—not just in doing what is good and true and beautiful according to God's law but also in suffering for rebellious sinners, the righteous laying down His life for the wicked, for their salvation.

Thus, God's will was perfectly done on earth as it was in heaven in the life, death, and resurrection of Jesus Christ: the law of God was perfectly observed in the sinless life of Jesus Christ; the justice of God was fully satisfied in the atoning death of Jesus

Christ for all the sins of His people. Jesus' resurrection testifies to His perfect righteousness as well as to His perfect atonement.

God's Will in Us

And God's will is done in all of us, who trust Jesus to be their Savior. This is certainly not because we ourselves have carried out God's law to perfection. We know that is far from the truth. But when we put our faith in Jesus Christ, God looks upon us "as if we had never sinned"—because Christ paid the full penalty of all our sins as our Substitute—and "as if we had fulfilled all of His commandments"—because Christ lived a life of perfect obedience to God's law as our Representative.

Sadly, of course, as long as we live in this fallen world in our sinful flesh, we will not be able to do God's will perfectly. But God's will, which is already done on account of what Christ has done *for* us (our justification), will one day be done on account of what Christ will complete *in* us (our glorification), even as He works out His will *in* us now, both to will and to work for His good pleasure (our sanctification). So then, let us devote ourselves to doing the will of God, which has been clearly revealed to us in His word! To this end, Christ has given us the Holy Spirit, who makes the means of grace efficacious and thereby enables us to do His will.

"Give Us This Day"
(Jesus, the Bread of Tomorrow)

From the "Your-petitions" to the "Us-petitions"

The petitions of the Lord's Prayer are not a random catalogue of independent, unrelated petitions. As we have seen already, they are organized and divided into two groups: the "Your-petitions" and the "Us-petitions." The "Your-petitions" come first and the "Us-petitions" follow. There is a clear progression in the arrangement of these petitions. This arrangement gives primacy to God—to His name, His kingdom and His will. The Lord's Prayer is definitely a theocentric—that is, God-centered—prayer.

But the Lord's Prayer does not end with the "Your-petitions." Having affirmed the primacy of God and His glory, the prayer moves on to the "Us-petitions"—to *our* need for bread, for forgiveness of sins and for God's guidance and deliverance. How wonderful it is that the Lord should include *our* needs in the Lord's Prayer! God, who is zealous for His own glory, is also mindful of His people's needs. God never forgets us (Isa. 49:15). He does not abandon us (Heb. 13:5). He is always mindful of us and our condition (Ps 8:4).

"Us-petitions"—Reflections of Our True Needs

The "Us-petitions" of the Lord's Prayer remind us of our true condition as needy creatures. How needy we are, indeed! We are wholly dependent on our Creator for our life, our Sustainer for our provision, and our Redeemer for our redemption. Knowing our utterly dependent condition, our gracious Lord calls us to pray for our needs! How kind and gracious He is!

When we think about this, can we approach prayer merely as a religious duty that we begrudgingly fulfill? Prayer is the divinely ordained means, by which we are allowed to approach the almighty, all-glorious God with our needs and desires! And to think that the almighty God is so mindful of our needs, so willing to listen to our petitions, that He should *command* us to pray! "O what peace we often forfeit, / O what needless pain we bear, / All because we do not carry / Everything to God in prayer!"

The Petitions of the Lord's Prayer and God's Covenant

As you can see, "Your-petitions" and "Us-petitions" are not independent of one another. They are closely related to one another. The context of the Lord's Prayer is the covenant relationship between God and His people, the union between the heavenly Father and His dear children. The glory of God cannot be separated from the satisfaction of His people's needs. And the needs of His people cannot be isolated from the glory of God. The "Us-petitions," then, flow from the "Your-petitions." In fact, the "Us-petitions" are the manifestation and realization of the "Your-petitions." The "Us-petitions" show what happens to us when God's name is hallowed, when the kingdom of God comes, and when the will of God is done on earth as it is in heaven.

The Unique Construction of the Fourth Petition

The "Us-petitions" begin with the fourth petition, "Give us this day our daily bread." This petition is unique in its construction.[12] To see this, we must translate the Greek in its original word order. When we do, we have:

Our Father in heaven,

Hallowed be Your name. (V+N)
Come Your kingdom. (V+N)
Be done Your will as in heaven also on earth. (V+N)

Our (daily) bread *give* us today. (N+V)
And *forgive* us our debts as we have forgiven our debtors. (V+N)
And *do not lead* us into temptation, (V+N)
But *deliver* us from evil. (V+N)

As you can see, all other petitions begin with a verb or a verbal phrase: "Hallowed be"; "Come"; "Be done"; "And forgive"; "And do not lead"; "But deliver." Only in this fourth petition do we begin with a noun, the direct object of the verb: "*Our (daily) bread* give us today." The steady beat of verb-noun, verb-noun, verb-noun is broken and we have in this petition a reversed word order: noun-verb. This variation in structure is designed to catch our attention and it is indeed for emphasis. And the emphasis falls on the noun phrase, "our daily bread," which is brought out to the front (unlike the other petitions).

That noun phrase sticks out even more because it has an added attributive adjective—"daily." The previous petitions simply had

12 Ernst Lohmeyer, *"Our Father": an Introduction to the Lord's Prayer* (John Bowden, Trans.). New York: Harper & Row, 1965), p. 134.

"You name," "Your kingdom," and "Your will." Here in the fourth petition we do not just have "our bread" but "our *daily* bread." So, this added adjective, "daily," receives emphasis and plays an important function in the petition.

Is This Petition about Food?

This petition seems to address the most basic need that we have: food. Living in the most affluent nation of the world, what most of us worry about is not so much whether or not we have something to eat today as *what* we want to eat among so many choices we have. But this petition for bread reminds us who the true Provider is. We may plant, we may water, and we may even fertilize and genetically engineer; but it is the Lord, who causes the growth. It is God, who causes the sun to rise and the rain to fall to make things grow for our food.

Earlier in the Sermon on the Mount, Jesus presented God as our heavenly Father, who provides for us: "But I say to you, love your enemies, and pray for those who persecute you in order that you may be sons of your Father who is in heaven; for He causes His sun to rise on *the* evil and *the* good, and sends rain on *the* righteous and *the* unrighteous" (Matt. 5:44-45). And Jesus prefaced the Lord's Prayer by saying, "[Y]our heavenly Father knows what you need before you ask Him" (6:8b). God feeds the birds of the air, though they do not sow, nor reap, nor gather into barns (6:26). If so, how much more will God do for His people, who are worth so much more than they, Jesus asked? So, Jesus declared, "Ask, and it shall be given to you; seek, and you shall find; knock, and it shall be opened to you. For everyone who asks receives, and he who seeks finds, and to him who knocks it shall be opened" (Matthew 7:7-8). How can we be so bold in our prayer? Jesus said, "If you then, being evil, know how to give good gifts to your children, how much more shall your Father who is in heaven give what is good to those who ask Him" (Matthew 7:11)! So, we can pray, "Give us this day our daily bread."

Jesus' Other Words about Asking for Bread

However, there are certain contextual considerations that make us go beyond this understanding of the fourth petition. Consider first what Jesus says later in the same chapter:

> "Do not be anxious then, saying, 'What shall we eat?' or 'What shall we drink?' or 'With what shall we clothe ourselves?' For all these things the Gentiles eagerly seek; for your heavenly Father knows that you need all these things. But seek first His kingdom and His righteousness; and all these things shall be added to you" (Matthew 6:31-33).

Jesus exhorts the disciples not to be like the Gentiles, who eagerly seek what to eat, what to drink, and what to wear. His disciples should seek first God's kingdom and His righteousness. Add to this what Jesus says in one of the Beatitudes: "Blessed are those who hunger and thirst for righteousness, for they shall be satisfied" (5:6). Here, the hunger of the blessed people is for righteousness rather than for bread. Also, Moses tells us in Deut. 8:3 what God desired the Israelites to learn during their forty-year wilderness journey: "And he humbled you and let you hunger and fed you with manna, which you did not know, nor did your fathers know, that he might make you know that man does not live by bread alone, but man lives by every word that comes from the mouth of the LORD."

Daily Bread?

These factors give us a sufficient reason to examine more closely what the fourth petition actually means. Indeed, we realize that the adjective translated as "daily" is quite enigmatic. The Greek word used is *epiousion*. This word is quite rare in the Greek New Testament. In fact, it occurs only twice, both in two different versions of the Lord's Prayer in Matthew and Luke. It does not occur at all in the Greek version of the Old Testament or in the extra biblical Greek literature. So, we don't have any outside help to determine the meaning of this word.

Etymologically there are three possible meanings. In most translations, the word is translated as "daily." However, if you look at the marginal note in your Bibles, you will see that other options are offered as viable translations: "our *needful* bread" or "our bread *for the coming day*." Can we determine which one is the right translation?

How about "the Bread of Tomorrow"?

Jehoachim Jeremias says, "In my opinion, the decisive fact is that the church father Jerome... tells us that in the lost Aramaic *Gospel of the Nazarenes* the term *mahar* appears, meaning 'tomorrow,' that here therefore the reference was to bread 'for tomorrow.'"[13] This fact becomes significant, considering that Aramaic was the language that was spoken in Palestine during Jesus' time. What is interesting is that Jesus speaks of "tomorrow" later in the same chapter: "Therefore do not be anxious for *tomorrow*; for tomorrow will care for itself. Each day has enough trouble of its own" (6:34). But the word used in v. 34 is not *epiousion* but *aurion*, which is a more commonly used Greek word for "tomorrow." It is very

---

13 Johachim Jeremias, *The Lord's Prayer* (Philadelphia: Fortress Press, 1973), p. 23.

possible that both words are translations of the same Aramaic word, *mahar*, which means "tomorrow."

However, by translating the same Hebrew word into two different Greek words, Matthew wanted to make a distinction between the two uses (Matt. 6:11 and Matt. 6:34). Since *aurion* is a more common word for tomorrow, we may conclude that Matthew wanted to use the word *epiousion* to mean something other than just the next 24-hour day. It is observed by Jeremias that, in the prophetic, apocalyptic literature of the intertestamental period, the Hebrew word *mahar* took on an eschatological dimension to mean the age to come.[14] If so, "the bread of tomorrow" in the Lord's Prayer must not mean the bread of the next day but the bread of the age to come, of the eschatological future. The translation of the fourth petition would then be, "The bread of tomorrow (or, the bread of the age to come), give us today." In this petition, then, Jesus brings two ages together—or, to be more precise, Jesus brings the future eschatological age into the present so that the two ages *overlap* with each other.

This Petition and the Giving of Manna on the Sixth Day

I believe that the most intriguing and compelling reason for this translation is provided by Charles Dennison, who saw the pattern of this petition in the double portion of manna given on the sixth day.[15] As you remember, the bread of the seventh day was given on the sixth day for Sabbath keeping. So then, from the perspective of the sixth day, the bread of the next day (tomorrow) was given to Israel on the sixth day ("this day").

---

14 Johachim Jeremias, *The Lord's Prayer* (Philadelphia: Fortress Press, 1973), pp. 23-24.

15 This insight was conveyed to me by Scott Sanborn, a former member of our church.

Take note of the specific focus of this evidence. The fourth petition, "The bread of tomorrow, give us today," cannot be prayed on the first five days of the week. Only on the sixth day can we pray for the manna of the next day, the bread of tomorrow. The fourth petition of the Lord's Prayer places us, then, in the sixth day. Isn't this interesting? What does this mean?

The Sixth Day of Redemptive History

Through the fourth petition, the Lord is declaring to His disciples that the sixth day in the redemptive calendar of God, the sixth day in the week of redemptive history, has arrived. This sixth day, of course, is an epochal designation: it refers to the age that we live in, not the sixth 24-hour day of our weekly calendar. Whether it is Monday or Tuesday, Saturday or Sunday, no matter what day it is in our weekly calendar, we are living in the sixth day of redemptive history.

What is the significance of this sixth day? It is the day before the seventh day. From the beginning, the seventh day was a special day set apart from the other days of the week: "on the seventh day God finished his work that he had done, and he rested on the seventh day from all his work that he had done. So God blessed the seventh day and made it holy…" (Gen. 2:2-3). Many have observed that only the seventh day of creation does not have the refrain of "there was evening and there was morning" attached at the end. It is as though God had entered His *eternal* rest. So, many saw the seven-day creation week as the pattern for history, which will enter into God's eternal rest on "the seventh day" of history. In fact, the Hebrews writer presents our ultimate Sabbath rest as entering God's (eternal) rest from His work on the seventh day (Heb. 4:9-10).

Interestingly, the manna that was given on the sixth day for the seventh day was extra special. Manna was a supernatural food. But the double portion of manna given on the sixth day was even more supernatural, if you will. While the manna of the other days perished after one day, the double portion of the manna given on the sixth day lasted for two days. This also points to the eschatological nature of the seventh day.

So then, the seventh day represents the age to come; the sixth day represents the end of this present age. The seventh day is of heaven; the sixth day is of the earth, the last epoch in human history, the last era of the first creation. The sixth day is "the last days," which are on the brink of the final destruction of the world. It is the age that will usher in the end of the world. *The fourth petition declares that the end of the world is near, that the end of the first creation is at hand!* The fourth petition declares that we are living in the last days, at the end of the world, on the sixth day of redemptive history! The fourth petition in effect says, "Repent, for the kingdom of heaven is at hand!" It calls us to wake up to the monumental, epochal changes that are about to take place. It calls us to be alert, watchful, and sober-minded. We are living in "the last days."

For Our Present Enjoyment of the Blessings of the Coming Age

The sixth day signifies another important truth: the bread of tomorrow, the bread of the age to come, the bread of heaven, is promised to us for our *present* enjoyment. For Jesus commands us to pray, "The bread of tomorrow, give us today!" Though tomorrow is yet to come, God desires to give us the bread of tomorrow today! The sixth day is the hinge between this present age and the age to come. On this sixth day of redemptive history, this present age and the age to come overlap. Even though it is still the sixth day, the power and reality of the seventh day intrudes into this day in the form of "the bread of tomorrow." Though our feet still touch the dusty ground of this world, our mouth is allowed to taste the bread of the seventh day, the bread from heaven, the bread of eternal nourishment.

Jesus, the Bread of Tomorrow

Then, what is the bread of tomorrow, for which we should pray? It cannot be denied that manna came from heaven. The people of Israel did not sow, they did not water, and they did not tend to it. It came right out of heaven and it was undoubtedly supernatural bread. As we saw, the manna they gathered on the sixth day was even more supernatural: it lasted into the seventh day while the manna of other days bred worms and became foul the next day. Yet, Jesus said to the Jews concerning the manna, "Your fathers ate the manna in the wilderness and they died" (John 6:49). Then, Jesus spoke of another kind of bread, even better than manna. Manna was but a sign. It pointed to the true Bread out of heaven. Jesus declared, "I am the living bread that came down out of heaven; if anyone eats of this bread, he shall live forever…" (John 6:51)!

Jesus is the Bread that came down out of heaven. Jesus is the Bread of the age to come, the age of eternity, the age of resurrection life. Jesus is the Bread of tomorrow given to us today, on this sixth day, in these last days of redemptive history. Like the manna of the seventh day given on the sixth day, so is Jesus, the true Bread of tomorrow, given to us on this day. All other bread is for daily sustenance. We eat and we grow hungry again. We eat and we still perish. But not with Jesus, the Bread of tomorrow. He nourishes us today with the strength and life of the age to come. He nourishes us with the Bread of life from heaven above as we journey through the wilderness of this world. Those who partake of Him shall live forever. Those who eat of this Bread of tomorrow shall not hunger for all eternity (John 6:35).

Again, we are reminded that what we pray for, what we long for, in the Lord's Prayer is the Lord Jesus Christ Himself. Shall we pray for anything less than that? Can we, born from above, desire anything less, anything other than, Jesus Christ Himself? Can our hearts be satisfied with anything less, anything other than, Jesus Christ when we are born again by the Spirit of Christ? What of this world can compare to the glory and beauty of Jesus Christ? "Fair is the sunshine, fair is the moonlight and all the twinkling starry host...." But "Jesus shines brighter, Jesus shines purer than all the angels heav'n can boast."

What of this world can satisfy you as Jesus can? Fair may be your spouse. Fair may be your dear children. Indeed, all that you enjoy in this world are God's gracious blessings on you and fair are all His temporal blessings. But remember: all the temporal blessings are temporary; they are for our daily sustenance, here today and gone tomorrow. They cannot be compared to Jesus Christ, who brought the bread of tomorrow—the eternal blessings of the age to come—into our present. He is our Living Bread, who will give us abundant, constant, eternal satisfaction that will never diminish but increase from abundance to abundance.

What We Should Hunger After

So then, our confession ought to be, "As a deer pants for flowing streams, so pants my soul for you, O God. My soul thirsts for God, for the living God..." (Ps. 42:1-2a). "Whom have I in heaven but you? And there is nothing on earth that I desire besides you" (Ps. 73:25). "I count everything as loss because of the surpassing worth of knowing Christ Jesus my Lord..." (Phil. 3:8a). In fact, our longing for Christ should be more intense since we are living in the last days. So James warns, "Come now, you rich, weep and howl for the miseries that are coming upon you. Your riches have rotted and your garments are moth-eaten. Your gold and silver have corroded, and their corrosion will be evidence against you and will eat your flesh like fire" (James 5:1-3b). Why such harsh words when all things are God's gifts to us? James goes on to say, "You have laid up treasure in the last days" (James 5:3c)!

It is always foolish to choose what is temporary over what is eternal, what is perishing over what is everlasting. But it is even more so in these last days when this present age is coming to an end, when the Bread of tomorrow is available today. This is not to say that the Old Testament saints did not have the *essence* of the Bread of tomorrow. Even during the first five days of the week, the people of Israel ate manna from heaven. In fact, the Old Testament saints received the same salvation as the new covenant believers do by trusting in God's promise for the Messiah. So, the Westminster Confession of Faith affirms, "The justification of believers under the Old Testament was, in all these respects, one and the same with the justification of believers under the New Testament" (11:6). But we have a far greater and fuller assurance because we have received the fulfillment of God's promise in the advent, life, death, and resurrection of Jesus Christ.

This greater assurance enhances our experience and enjoyment of the Bread of tomorrow all the more. His resurrection demonstrated, among many things, that the kingdom of heaven is not just an idea, or merely pie in the sky, but a reality—a reality more real than what we can see and touch, "For the things that are seen are transient, but the things that are unseen are eternal" (2 Cor. 4:18). Jesus' bodily resurrection unto eternal life is clearly a supernatural event, which defies all the laws of physics. It is a powerful evidence that this natural, materialistic world is not all there is to reality. A more powerful reality of supernatural, resurrection life, which is not subject to the force of death and decay, exists. Any worldview, which ignores this reality, is terribly truncated and misleading.

Waiting for the Seventh Day

This petition also challenges us to prepare with a greater sense of urgency for the full arrival of the seventh day in Jesus' Second Coming. It is true that He has not returned for the past two thousand years. Does that mean He is never coming back? It may be tempting to think that way sometimes. But if Jesus were to never return, it would negate everything Jesus said and did for our salvation. It would also mean that there is really no hope for true justice for all the evil and wickedness in the world. But if Jesus is not a liar and Christianity is not the greatest hoax in history, it just means that we are two thousand years closer to His Return. Of course, Jesus may not come back for another thousand years or hundred years or He may come back this year or tomorrow. He will come like a thief in the night when people don't expect. One thing is for sure: we must live in expectation of His Return. We must live like the students in the last week of school, who know that their final exams are just around the corner. If Christ should not return in our lifetime, we know that we shall go to Him after we die to be welcomed into our Father's house.

This fourth petition reminds us of the utter insufficiency of "the bread of this age" to truly satisfy us. This is not because the things of this world are evil and bad in and of themselves. They are God's good and gracious gifts to us. But they are not good enough for those who are made in God's image, who cannot live by bread alone but by every word that proceeds out of the mouth of God (Deut. 8:3). Even the best of this world is not worthy of those who are predestined for the surpassing riches of heaven. So then, let us rightly order our lives and our affections. We can, and we should, enjoy even the temporal gifts that God so graciously bestows on us, far beyond what we deserve. But we must not idolize them and make them the basis of our self-worth and happiness. God has granted to us the Bread of tomorrow, which alone can truly satisfy our deepest longings because it is none other than our Lord Jesus Christ. Let us be grateful for this wonderful Gift of God. Let us treasure our privilege to have a foretaste of the life-giving, life-transforming Bread of heaven and make It our chief delight—until we can have a full taste of It in heaven on that glorious day and for all eternity!

"Forgive Us Our Debts..."
(Jesus, Our Jubilee)

Our Accountability to God

"Forgive us our debts...." Who can pray this prayer? No one can pray it with any degree of sincerity if s/he does not accept our accountability to God. The ideas of forgiveness and debt do not exist apart from the reality of accountability.

Consciously or not so consciously, this has got to be one of the major reasons—if not *the* reason—that many want to do away with the existence of God. "Why do the nations rage and the peoples plot in vain? The kings of the earth set themselves, and the rulers take counsel together, against the LORD and against his anointed, saying, 'Let us burst their bonds apart and cast away their cords from us'" (Ps. 2:1-3)—the bonds and cords of moral accountability to God. If there is no God, if we are just a product of the mindless, purposeless, accidental evolutionary process, then we don't have to answer to God for our actions.

But if God is our Creator, who made us according to His purpose, it makes all the difference in the world. The meaning and purpose of our life cannot be something we make up as we go; they have been determined by our Creator even before we came into being. Ultimately, the success of our life is to be assessed by God's creational intent. Imagine a DVD with all kinds of valuable information being used as a coaster. What a waste!

Our Failure to Meet Our Obligations

This petition also presupposes that we have failed to meet our obligation to God. Thus the mention of "our debts." Indeed, we have incurred debts to God to such a degree that we cannot possibly pay them off. Thus the helpless plea, "*Forgive* us our debts!" This is why man in his sinful state tries to do away with his accountability to God, even if he must deny the existence of God altogether. Would it bother him so much if he met his obligation? If he did well, would he not look forward to the day of accounting? It would be his moment of vindication and glory—the divine Master saying to him, "Well done, My good and faithful servant! Enter into your Master's glory!"

It doesn't feel good to be indebted. Six months after finishing your higher education, you must start paying off your student loan. You see the total amount of your loan, how much you have to pay every month, and how long—how many years and even decades—it will take you to pay it off and finally be debt-free. Then, you purchase a house, too, and a big chunk of your income goes into paying off the mortgage, not to mention the property tax and (for some in California) Mella Roos tax! Until you pay off the mortgage, the house is really not yours. If you default on your loan, the house can be taken away! The pressure is high and many lose sleep over it.

But in these cases, we are only dealing with financial institutions. We do not have a personal relationship with them and our obligation is mostly financial in nature. But what about our debts to *God*? *What* do we owe Him?

What Do We Owe God?

Since God is our Maker, we owe Him our very lives and everything related to our living. Our body is His. Our soul is His. Our time is His. Our talents and gifts are His. So are our possessions and resources as well as our relationships. All these, the Lord has given to us. And all these, He can take away (Job 1:21). He can take away our lives this very moment—then, what will happen to all that we have (Luke 12:20)? It is not just our lives but all things are held together by Him (Col. 1:17). What we call gravity and electromagnetism and strong force and weak force are just scientific descriptions of God's power, by which He holds the whole universe together! If God should withdraw His hand of providence, this whole universe would collapse in an instant. We live and move and have our being in God (Acts 17:28).

Every breath we breathe, every ounce of energy we have, every talent we possess, every moment we live—we have all of them on loan from God. They are to be used for the glory of God according to His purpose. When we fail to honor God with and through them, we are stealing from God what is rightfully His.

Does this sound oppressive and offensive? Does it sound like the worst form of slavery? If so, it may very well be a sure proof of our fallen condition. If there is nothing we have that we have not received from God, if our life itself is given by God, can we deny God's total and complete lordship over us and every aspect of our life? Feeling the need to be free of God's lordship is an indication that something is seriously wrong with us—like a dog that bites the hand that feeds him! There is a compelling and obvious moral obligation we have toward God, from whom we receive our life and all our blessings.

Oh, how much we owe to God! Enormous are the debts we have incurred toward Him. Think of all the wasted opportunities for acknowledging God as God, giving Him thanks for all His benefits to us, and glorifying Him through our willing and joyful obedience to His will. Think of all the ways we have broken His law in thought, word, and deed. If you have ever been disrespected or ignored by someone under your authority, you know how infuriating it is. But what is *our* authority compared to the authority of *God*? How much more wicked it is to disrespect the infinite honor of God! If justice requires an eye for an eye and a tooth for a tooth, what do we owe to God for violating His *infinite* honor? A place of eternal torment is what we deserve. How grave are the consequences of our sins! How great our debts! Can we ever pay them back? All we can do is to ask for His forgiveness in total helplessness.

Why Divine Forgiveness is not so Simple

But divine forgiveness is not as simple as God simply choosing to forget about our debts because He was moved by our pitiful plea. Our debts to God are called trespasses, or sins, in v. 14. God, the foundation of whose throne is righteousness and justice (Ps. 89:14), cannot let any sin go unpunished (Ex. 34:7). So, He could not simply and arbitrarily cancel our debts. In order to cancel our debts, He had to nail them *to the cross*, the cross on which our Savior died to pay our debts (Col. 2:14). Without the costly sacrifice of God's eternal Son, the enormous debt we accrued—infinite, indeed, in its amount and gravity—cannot be done away with!

Again, when we ask God to forgive us, we are asking for Christ. Only Christ can pay for our debt with the infinite value of His life! There is no other way, there is no other plea, there is no other hope, than Jesus' blood and righteousness to do away with our debt to God! And our Savior was willing to pay our debts with His life: by His death we are forgiven!

Unique Features of This Petition

But we notice that this petition does not end there. This petition goes on to say, "as we forgive our debtors." Although each of the petitions in the Lord's Prayer is unique, this addition makes this petition even more so in a couple of ways.

First, it is only in this petition that we have human activity mentioned: "as *we* also forgive our debtors." All other petitions are wholly concerned with God's activity: it is God, who will hallow His own name, bring His heavenly kingdom, accomplish His sovereign will, give us our bread of tomorrow, lead us not into temptation and deliver us from evil. The fifth petition alone has our act of forgiveness as an integral part.

Second, only this petition is followed by an additional comment or explanation (vv. 14-15). It seems as though Jesus wanted to impress the significance of this petition in our minds as well as make the meaning of this petition clear.

What are We Praying for?

What does this petition mean? It is difficult not to be disturbed by the logical order of this petition: "Forgive us our debts *as we forgive our debtors!*" Shouldn't it be, "Help us to forgive our debtors as You have forgiven our debts"? Doesn't *that* accurately reflect the principle of grace, which is essential to our salvation and Christian life? "We love because he first loved us" (2 John 4:19). If we forgive—if we can, and must, forgive—it is because God has forgiven us first so freely in Jesus Christ. We don't forgive in order to earn God's forgiveness. Yet, that seems to be precisely the logic of Jesus' words. It reverses the logical order of the principle of grace, in which God's forgiveness comes first as the basis for our forgiveness of others.

As if to drive this point home, Jesus reinforces and explains in vv. 14-15 what He meant in this petition: "For if you forgive others their trespasses, your heavenly Father will also forgive you, but if you do not forgive others their trespasses, neither will your Father forgive your trespasses." In fact, Jesus does this only for this petition and not for any other! Is Jesus contradicting the very essence of His own gospel? Is He denouncing the principle of grace? We know that cannot be true. Then, why does He say what He says in this petition?

Forgiveness and the Year of Jubilee

Let us first notice Jesus' choice of words. Although He uses the term, "trespasses," in His later explanation, in the petition itself Jesus uses the term "debts." Jesus also speaks of our need to forgive others' "debts." These two occurrences of "debts" clearly point us to a very specific institution in the Old Testament.

In the Old Testament, the idea of forgiving others' debts was associated with the sabbatical year (Deut. 15:1-2). Every seventh year the Israelites were to forgive their debtors. As they did so, they were to proclaim, "Release to the Lord!" The seventh year was the year of forgiveness. So, Moses refers to the sabbatical year as the year of remission (of debts) (Deut. 31:10). But, of course, the Year of Jubilee was the crown of the year of remission. "On the Day of Atonement you shall sound the trumpet throughout all your land. And you shall consecrate the fiftieth year, and proclaim liberty throughout the land to all its inhabitants. It shall be a jubilee for you, when each of you shall return to his property and each of you shall return to his clan" (Lev. 25:9-10).

It seems that Jesus had the Year of Jubilee in mind when He was teaching His disciples to pray this petition. What is Jesus signaling by doing so? He is declaring that the true Year of Jubilee has arrived! For it is time for us to forgive one another's debts! So, the stress is placed on *our* forgiveness of others' debts!

The Day of Atonement and the Year of Jubilee

How appropriate it was that the Old Testament Year of Jubilee should begin on the Day of Atonement! The Day of Atonement was the day for Israel's annual atonement for its sins. It was the day when the Lord remitted (or, sent away) Israel's debt. And it was on the Day of Atonement in the seventh sabbatical year that the Year of Jubilee began—the year of great release, the year of great remission, the year of great forgiveness! Each Jew regained his inheritance in the Year of Jubilee. Each Jew regained his freedom and returned to his family in the Year of Jubilee. Why? The Lord declared, "For they are my servants, whom I brought out of the land of Egypt; they shall not be sold as slaves" (Lev. 25:42); "The land shall not be sold in perpetuity, for the land is mine. For you are strangers and sojourners with me" (Lev. 25:23).

As you can see, the sons of Israel were to imitate their God by obeying these statutes. As the Lord gave them rest in the land, they were to give rest to their debtors by remitting their debts in the sabbatical year, especially in the Year of Jubilee. This was to remind them of God's sovereign ownership over them. They were stewards of the Lord of heaven and earth. Whatever they had was graciously and generously given to them by God for their enjoyment. But they were not to forget that everything they had belonged ultimately to God. They were to remember this every seventh year, especially in the Year of Jubilee, and forgive the debts of their countrymen.

So then, in teaching us to pray this prayer, Jesus is not denying the principle of grace. He is in fact building on the principle of grace. With this petition, Jesus highlights the absolute necessity of forgiving others as the only proper response to God's forgiving grace. Isn't this the exact point of Jesus' Parable of the Unforgiving Servant (Matt. 18:23-35)? In it, the master rebukes the unforgiving servant with these words: "You wicked servant! I forgave you all that debt because you pleaded with me. And should not you have had mercy on your fellow servant, as I had mercy on you" (18:32-33)? Jesus concludes the parable by saying, "And in anger his master delivered him to the jailers, until he should pay all his debt. So also my heavenly Father will do to every one of you, if you do not forgive your brother from your heart" (18:34-35).

This parable shows, in the same spirit as the petition in view, the necessary and inseparable connection between God's forgiveness of our sins and our forgiveness of others' sins. Simply put, the moment we receive God's gracious forgiveness in Jesus Christ, we have given up the right not to forgive others. The parable shows how reprehensible it is to receive God's great forgiveness and refuse to extend our small forgiveness to our fellow sinners. It is this message Jesus communicates through the wording of the petition in view.

Can You be a Christian and Not Forgive Others?

How we need this reminder! Forgiveness is one of the most difficult things to do. A sure sign of Christian maturity is the willingness and ability to forgive others. A sure sign of a mature congregation is genuine reconciliation among its members after a conflict.

But the words of our Lord seem to say more: willingness to forgive is an indispensable sign of being a disciple of Jesus Christ. In other words, someone who is unwilling to forgive is no Christian at all! Consider what Jesus once told the disciples in this regard: "If your brother sins, rebuke him, and if he repents, forgive him, and if he sins against you seven times in the day, and turns to you seven times, saying, 'I repent,' you must forgive him" (Luke 17:3-4). Hearing this, the disciples said, "Increase our faith" (Luke 17:5)! But what did Jesus say in response? "If you had faith like a grain of mustard seed, you could say to this mulberry tree, 'Be uprooted and planted in the sea,' and it would obey you" (Luke 17:6). What did Jesus mean by that? He seems to be saying that, even if we had the smallest of faith like a mustard seed, we should be able to forgive others seven times a day—that is, even the weakest Christian, if he is a Christian indeed, should be able to do so.

Forgiving by Faith, not by Will

It is not that a person cannot be a Christian until he develops enough willpower to forgive others. Jesus spoke of *faith*, not of *willpower*. This is not to say that faith has nothing to do with our will, of course. Faith is more than just (intellectually) knowing that Jesus is our Savior; faith involves the volitional aspect of trusting Jesus to save us. But faith has its focus on its object— who it is that we trust—not on the will.

What, then, does it mean to forgive by faith and not by will? The way we forgive others is not by trying to minimize or rationalize their offense, which is a form of psychological manipulation. Nor is it by reminding ourselves, "Not forgiving someone is like drinking poison and expecting the other person to die." This is a wholly self-centered approach. The way we forgive is by going back to the cross and seeing what Christ had to do to forgive *us*, whose sins are too many to count, too horrible to recount. It is in seeing Christ by faith that we are moved to forgive.

This is not to say that forgiveness is easy. But a Christian is not someone who says, "Well, it will take a long time for me to forgive you. So, don't expect me to forgive you any time soon." A Christian is someone who recognizes that he *must* forgive. We cannot receive God's free and complete and immediate forgiveness in Jesus Christ and still hold on to our "right" not to forgive, or to take as long as we need to feel like we can forgive.

What Forgiveness is

One of the reasons that people find it difficult to forgive is because they misunderstand what forgiveness is. They think that forgiving is forgetting, that they must *feel* like forgiving without any sense of resentment or any memory of pain. But forgiveness is rather a *promise* we make, summarized in the jingle, "Good thoughts, hurt you not, gossip never, friends forever."[16] Even when we don't feel like forgiving, even when we may still be reeling under pain, we can make this promise for the sake of Christ, can't we? We can and we must.

In fact, Jesus warns us that, if anyone is not willing to forgive others, he should not expect God to forgive him. His unwillingness to forgive may be an evidence that he may have never truly experienced God's forgiveness. Here, I'm talking about someone

16 Ken Sande, *The Peacemaker* (Grand Rapids: Baker Books, 2004), p. 209, quoting Corlette Sande, *The Young Peacemaker*.

"unwilling" to forgive, not someone having difficulty forgiving. We should not expect forgiving others to be easy, especially when the offense is grave. But it is one thing to have difficulty forgiving (because we know we must forgive while our heart may still be bleeding) and another to simply refuse to forgive (as if we had the right not to forgive). This petition shows how serious our Lord is in expecting us to forgive one another. He is not doing this to make our lives difficult. Rather, He is doing this to deepen our understanding and appreciation of His amazing grace. If we find it difficult to forgive others' small offenses, how much more difficult it must have been for a holy God! How great must be His love to lay down His life for sinners like us to grant us free forgiveness!

Experiencing God's Forgiveness by Forgiving Others

There is also an experiential dimension to this petition. There is a strong sense in which we do not experience the relief and joy of God's forgiveness until we forgive those who have sinned against us. Here, we are not talking about the once-for-all forgiveness we have already received in our justification. Objectively speaking, the moment we place our faith in Jesus Christ, all of our sins are washed away by the precious blood of Jesus Christ—"not in part but the whole." But we are still called to confess our sins throughout our Christian life and, when we do, we personally *experience* God's forgiveness (1 John 1:9). This is something we cannot enjoy as long as we refuse to forgive others as we are commanded to do.

A Call for Humility

This petition also calls for our deep humility. Think about what we should do when we do readily forgive others. Can we demand, "Since we forgave our debtors, You should forgive us"? Not at all!

Jesus tells us to plead for God's forgiveness even as we forgive our debtors. We do not earn God's forgiveness by forgiving others. After forgiving all who have sinned against us, we can only confess before God, "We are unworthy servants; we have only done what was our duty" (Luke 17:10). As those who have been saved by Christ's sacrificial love, it is our duty not only to forgive all who have sinned against us but also to love them as we love ourselves. Extending forgiveness to one another is the least we can do. So then, after forgiving others, we should still humbly pray for God's forgiveness.

Again, this is a powerful demonstration of the principle of grace at work ("I forgave you all that debt because you pleaded with me. And should not you have had mercy on your fellow servant, as I had mercy on you" [Matt. 18:33]?). We cannot receive God's grace and refuse to extend grace to others without weakening our assurance of salvation and our fellowship with God.

Jesus our Jubilee!

Let us remember that "Jesus is the Jubilee"[17] and the Year of Jubilee has arrived in His coming! It began when Jesus died on the cross, on the ultimate Day of Atonement for all our sins! It is time for us to forgive one another! Let the jubilation of Jubilee increase as we offer forgiveness to one another in Jesus Christ! For when we forgive, our assurance of God's forgiveness will increase and deepen ever more. What about the damage to our relationships caused by sin? Our damaged relationships can never go back to the way they used to be. But they can be made stronger when we forgive one another by the power of the gospel—until we will live in perfect peace with God and with one another in heaven forever!

---

17 Michael Card, "Jubilee."

"Lead Us Not Into Temptation..."
(Jesus, the Overcomer)

"Lead us not into temptation but deliver us from evil." This is the sixth and the last petition of the Lord's Prayer. We will treat this as one petition with two sub-petitions. Ultimately, the two sub-petitions are about the same thing. But before we take a detailed look at this petition, let us settle some preliminary questions.

Temptation or *Test?*

Let's first examine the Greek word translated as "temptation." The Greek word for temptation (*peirasmos*) can be translated also as "test/trial" (Gal. 4:14; Heb. 3:8). The same is true of its verbal form (*peirazo*): it can be translated as either "tempt" or "test/try." Its usage, then, should be determined by its context.

For our purposes here, we can generally say that the usage of this word depends largely on who is doing the act: God *tests* whereas Satan *tempts*. God does not temp because to tempt is to prompt, persuade, or entice someone to sin. It is unthinkable that a holy God should tempt us to sin. So, James declares that God is without temptation (*apeirastos*) (1:13)—that is, God does not tempt us. But to test, or to put through trial, is to bring to light the true nature or character of something/someone. This, God does. The Bible clearly states that God did *peirazo* Abraham (Gen. 22:1, LXX) as well as the Israelites in the wilderness (Deut. 8:2, LXX)—that is, God *tested* Abraham and Israel. So then, there is a way in which God does not *peirazo* (tempt)—that is what Satan does for our destruction—and there is another way in which God does *peirazo* (test)—this is what God does for our edification.

Our Experience—Test *and* Temptation

The dual meaning of this word aptly reflects the dual reality of our experience: what we experience may be both a test and a temptation at the same time. Think about Job's situation. He was tempted by Satan to curse God to His face (Job 1:11). But can we say that he was not being tested by God? In a sense, Job's experience was a trial by ordeal, by which he was to demonstrate his loyalty to God.[18] Consider what set the whole ordeal in motion. God told Satan, "Have you considered my servant Job, that there is none like him on the earth, a blameless and upright man, who fears God and turns away from evil" (Job 1:8)? God was daring Satan to challenge His champion, Job.

We can say something similar about what we face every day. When we feel tempted to sin, we should not think that God is absent in that situation. Every temptation we face can also be God's test to see whether we will stay faithful and loyal to Him. This is so because God is sovereign. Nothing happens outside His sovereign control, including Satan's temptation. Joseph told his terrified brothers, "As for you, you meant evil against me, but

---

18 M.G. Kline, "Trial by Ordeal" in *Through Christ's Word: a Festschrift for Dr. Philip E. Hughes*, ed. by W. Robert Godfrey, Jesse L. Boyd III. Phillipsburg, NJ: Presbyterian and Reformed, 1985, p. 86.

God meant it for good, to bring it about that many people should be kept alive, as they are today" (Gen. 50:20). We can also say, "Satan means evil against us and tempts us all the time but God means it for our good, working all things together for the good of those who love Him and are called according to His purpose."

Lead Us not into Test?

So, how should the Greek word be translated in the sixth petition? Is it, "Lead us not into *temptation*" or "Lead us not into *test/trial*"?

We may say that the translation should be, "Lead us not into test/trial," because God does not tempt. Why should we ask God not to do something that He doesn't intend to do anyway? But God does test. He tested Abraham and He tested the Israelites in the wilderness. So, it makes sense to pray, "Lead us not into test/trial."

But that doesn't make sense, either. Why does God test His people in the first place? He does it for our good, for our edification. Indeed, the New Testament consistently emphasizes the positive function of trial in Christian life:

> "Count it all joy, my brothers, when you meet trials of various kinds, for you know that the testing of your faith produces steadfastness. And let steadfastness have its full effect, that you may be perfect and complete, lacking in nothing" (James 1:2-4);

> "Blessed is the man who remains steadfast under trial, for when he has stood the test he will receive the crown of life, which God has promised to those who love him" (James 1:12);

"In this you rejoice, though now for a little while, if necessary, you have been grieved by various trials, so that the tested genuineness of your faith—more precious than gold that perishes though it is tested by fire-- may be found to result in praise and glory and honor at the revelation of Jesus Christ" (1 Pet. 1:6-7).

Trials are not pleasant. But they are not to be avoided at all cost because they are designed to strengthen our faith and purify our hope as a refiner's fire. God uses them to wean us from the world, which is perishing away. If so, why should we ask God to remove all tests and trials from our lives?

Lead Us not into Temptation?

But what about, "Lead us not into temptation"? This translation has an obvious problem. James declares simply and forcefully that God does not tempt anyone: "Let no one say when he is tempted, 'I am being tempted by God,' for God cannot be tempted with evil, and he himself tempts no one" (James 1:13). If God does not tempt anyone, why should we ask God not to lead us into temptation? Isn't this like a child begging his parents everyday, "Please don't hate me!" Of course, hating his own child would be the last thing any parent in his right mind would do! To plead the parents again and again not to hate him would be an insult to them. Are we doing the same thing when we ask God not to lead us into temptation?

But if we use that logic, all the petitions of the Lord's Prayer would be unnecessary. God will hallow his name and there is no chance both in heaven and earth that He will fail to do so. God's kingdom will come and nothing can stop Him from bringing His kingdom in its full glory. You get the idea, don't you? God's sovereign will shall be done. God's greatest desire is to give His children the Bread of tomorrow. God will gladly forgive the debts of His children as they forgive their debtors. That these things will happen is more certain than the fact that we are here. Nothing can prevent God from accomplishing His purpose (Isa. 46:10-11). Then why should we pray these petitions? Are they totally unnecessary because God will do them anyway? Is it silly to ask God not to do something that He will never do?

Praying According to God's Will

But that is precisely the point of the Lord's Prayer. Jesus is teaching us *to pray according to God's will*. If our prayer is an expression of our deepest desire, praying according to God's will is a powerful way to conform our will to His. By teaching us what God's will is through the Lord's Prayer and calling us to pray it, Jesus intends to conform our will and desire to God's heart.

We have been saying all along that the ultimate answer to the Lord's Prayer is the Lord Jesus Christ Himself, specifically as our *Savior*. But what is salvation? It is salvation particularly from sin (Matt. 1:21). But in speaking of salvation, we cannot just speak of what we are saved from; we must also speak of what we are saved unto. A prisoner may want nothing more than getting out of jail. But once he gets out of jail, then what? He must think about how he is going to live and for what. The forgiveness of sin, as crucial as it is, is not all there is to our salvation. It may spare us from the punishment of sin but we must also deal with the power of sin as well as the presence of sin. That is why our salvation does not just consist of justification (by which we are delivered from the punishment of sin) but also of sanctification (by which we are being delivered from the power of sin) and glorification (by which we will be delivered from the presence of sin).

But what is implied above must be stated clearly: we need to be free from sin so that we can be conformed to God and His will—this is ultimately what our sanctification and glorification are about. Our Lord intended our will and desire to conform to those of God as we pray according to His will, as we pray the Lord's Prayer. So, we should not feel uneasy in praying, "Lead us not into temptation…." God's will is not to lead us into temptation. So, we are to pray according to His will.

A Call for Humility

This petition calls for a humble acknowledgment of our weaknesses. By it we confess that we are vulnerable and susceptible to temptation, that we are easily led into temptation, that we are an easy prey to temptation. Because of the Fall, we were all brought forth in iniquity and conceived in sin (Ps. 51:5). We may not be as evil as we can be but we are corrupt in every aspect of our being. Our heart is a cup of water polluted with drops of deadly venom. Everything that we do is tainted by the poison of sin. Every intent of the thoughts of our heart is only evil continually (Gen. 6:5). Out of the heart flow evil thoughts, murders, adulteries, fornications, thefts, false witness, and slanders (Matt. 15:19).

So, the cobra of our sinful nature raises its ugly head at the first note of a seductive tune. The tempter need not shout but only whisper and he will find the most willing audience in us. At the wink of his crafty eyes, the lust of the flesh, the lust of the eyes, and the boastful pride of life will break loose and wreak havoc in our restless, inconstant soul. Just one glimpse at a lewd image is enough to hook our curiosity and drag us into a downward spiral of sexual immorality in thoughts and actions. One unkind word or even a wrong tone of voice can thrust us into a sudden eruption of anger. When there is no apparent danger of being caught, we will steal and cheat, embezzle and loot. When put on the spot, we will lie and fabricate with no regard for later just to avoid the embarrassment of the moment. We salivate when we hear gossip, eager to entertain ourselves at the expense of others with little regard for their name and character. Oh, how easily we are tempted! Oh, how easily we sin when tempted! Oh, how we need to pray, "Lead us not into temptation!" Oh, how we need to pray, "Deliver us from evil!" So weak and helpless we are!

A Bold Acknowledgment of God's Sovereignty

But this petition is also our bold acknowledgment of God's sovereignty. In praying, "Deliver us from evil," we acknowledge that God is able to deliver us from evil even though we cannot deliver ourselves from evil—so drenched in evil we are. And in praying, "Lead us not into temptation," we acknowledge that not even one temptation can take place outside of God's sovereign will. As the Westminster Shorter Catechism teaches, God preserves and governs *all His creatures* as well as *all their actions* by His most holy, wise and powerful will (A. 11). Nothing happens apart from God's will. Not even a bird falls from the sky unless God permits it. Even Satan cannot do anything without God's permission. Did we not see this in what happened to Job? Satan could not go one nanometer beyond the boundary that God set down for him in tempting Job to curse God and die.

What encouragement and comfort this assurance provides for us! Even temptations are not outside of God's sovereign control, who works all things according to the counsel of His will (Eph. 1:11)! Though He allows evil to take place, He is able to work all things together—including evil and temptations—for the good of those who love Him and are called according to His purpose (Rom. 8:28).

The Ultimate Temptation and Evil—Apostasy

But there is one temptation, one evil, which we must pray that God will never permit in our lives. What we are really praying against in the sixth petition is the kind of temptation that will lead to apostasy, the ultimate evil. Consider what Jesus says in Rev. 3:10 in this regard. There Jesus says to the church in Philadelphia, "Because you have kept my word about patient endurance, I will keep you from the hour of trial that is coming on the whole world, to try those who dwell on the earth." The word translated here in ESV as "trial" is, of course, *peirasmos*, which can also be translated as "temptation." So, "the hour of trial" can be translated also as "the hour of temptation." The latter seems more appropriate, given that "the hour" is for the destruction of "those who dwell on the earth".

Who are "those who dwell upon the earth" in Revelation? The phrase does not refer to all people; it refers to the people who are contrasted with, and distinguished from, those who belong to the Lamb, who stand on Mount Zion, whose names are written in the book of life, etc. So, we have in Revelation 13:8, "...*all who dwell on earth* will worship [the beast], everyone whose name has not been written before the foundation of the world in the book of life of the Lamb who was slain." Unbelievers are described as "all that dwell upon the earth" because they are earthly-minded. They have no concern, no interest in, the things of God or heaven. And they will face the hour of temptation and they will perish along with Satan and his minions.

Here Jesus is promising the Christians in Philadelphia and all Christians that He will spare them from the kind of temptation that will lead to eternal damnation. What we have in the sixth petition as a prayer ("Lead us not into temptation"), we have in Rev. 3:10 as a promise ("I will keep you from the hour of temptation"). This was a promise not just for the end of the world. It was given to the Christians in Philadelphia as well as to all Christians who live between the First Coming and the Second Coming of Jesus Christ. For this temptation always lurks around Christians: "Be sober-minded; be watchful. Your adversary the devil prowls around like a roaring lion, seeking someone to devour" (1 Pet. 5:8).

Jesus the Overcomer

On what basis, then, will God's people be protected from the hour of temptation? Not too far from our text, we read in Matt. 4:1, "Then Jesus was led up by the Spirit into the wilderness to be tempted by the devil." The word "led" here is different from the word "lead" in the sixth petition. But the idea is the same. Here we see Jesus Christ being led into the wilderness to be tempted by Satan. And Satan tempts Him as he did the first Adam. Adam was tempted with the lust of the flesh ("the tree was good for food"), with the lust of the eyes ("it was pleasant to the eyes"), and with the boastful pride of life ("the tree was desirable to make one wise"). So was Jesus, the last Adam, tempted with the lust of the flesh ("command that these stoned become bread"), with the lust of the eyes ("the devil took him to a very high mountain and *showed him* all the kingdoms of the world and their glory"), and with the boastful pride of life ("He will command his angels concerning you.... On their hands they will bear you up, lest you strike your foot against a stone [because you are supposed to be so important]").

But whereas the first Adam failed, the last Adam succeeded. Jesus overcame the temptations of Satan and did not sin. Jesus refused to worship Satan for the lust of the eyes. Jesus refused to test the

Lord by jumping off the pinnacle of the temple. Jesus affirmed, even after fasting forty days and nights, that "man does not live by bread alone, but man lives by every word that comes from the mouth of the LORD" (Deut. 8:3).

Here, we hear the echoes of Israel's wilderness journey. God characterized it as a time of testing:

> "…the LORD your God has led you these forty years in the wilderness, that he might humble you, testing you to know what was in your heart, whether you would keep his commandments or not. And he humbled you and let you hunger and fed you with manna, which you did not know, nor did your fathers know, that he might make you know that man does not live by bread alone, but man lives by every word that comes from the mouth of the LORD" (Deut. 8:2-3).

You can see how Jesus is not only the last Adam but also the true Israel, who succeeded where Adam and Israel failed so miserably.

Jesus was again tempted in the garden of Gethsemane, this time directly dealing with the most critical matter concerning our redemption—His messianic mission as the suffering Servant of the Lord to bear the guilt of our sin. There, too, He was tempted three times. Three times He prayed, "My Father, if it be possible, let this cup pass from me…." But each time He resisted the temptation and prayed, "…nevertheless, not as I will, but as you will" (Matt. 26:39).

And it is because of Him, "who in every respect has been tempted as we are, yet without sin" (Heb. 4:15), we are spared from the hour of temptation. We will not be found alone in our weakness and sinfulness in the hour of temptation. Christ the righteous, Christ the impeccable and incorruptible, is our Shelter and Refuge. We may falter and fail at times. We may suffer the *natural* and *moral* consequences of our sins in this life. But they are not God's *judicial punishment* for our sins. For He, who overcame all temptations, have also laid down His life for us and our sins. "Therefore, there is no condemnation for those who are in Christ Jesus" (Rom. 8:1).

Our Glorious End

As we bring to an end our reflection on this final petition of the Lord's Prayer, let us look to the ultimate end—our eternal life in heaven. Keeping the end in view is a good approach to understanding the meaning of God's Word—just as the meaning and purpose of each part of a story should be understood in light of the ending. God, after all, is the One who declares "the end from the beginning, and from ancient times things which have not been done" (Isa. 46:10). God does not do anything haphazardly, out of whim, in reaction to something unexpected. To an all-knowing, sovereign God, nothing is unexpected. Indeed, He has predestined all things. Everything God does in history is intentional and purposeful, designed to achieve His final goal. Everything God does, He does it for His glory. And God is most glorified when He saves His people and judges the wicked and unrepentant. God's ultimate glory will be revealed on the Day of Judgment.

On that day, God will expose all the secret thoughts and deeds of the wicked and declare their guilt. In horror they will cry out to the mountains and to the rocks, "Fall on us and hide us from the presence of Him who sits on the throne, and from the wrath of the Lamb; for the great day of their wrath has come; and who is able to stand" (Rev. 6:16-17)? And God will punish them for their sin against His infinite honor, for their rejection of His grace in Jesus Christ, the one and only Savior. They will be cast out from the light of His glory into the outer darkness, where there shall be weeping and gnashing of teeth. They will be thrown into the lake of fire to be tormented for all eternity.

And on that day, God will vindicate His people in Jesus Christ and recompense all their sufferings for Christ. They will enter the new heaven and the new earth, the new Jerusalem, to dwell with God forever. God will "wipe away every tear from their eyes, and death shall be no more, neither shall there be mourning, nor crying, nor pain anymore..." (Rev. 21:4). There in heaven all will be peace and joy and love forever, full of goodness, truth, and beauty.

When that day of salvation comes, we shall finally be free—completely!—from our sin and its dreadful consequences. We shall sin no more. There will be no desire in us to sin, for we shall all be glorified: we will not be able to sin! And when we are finally and fully free from our sinful nature, we will have advanced beyond Adam's innocence before the Fall. From his state of innocence ("able to sin"), he was to advance into the state of glory where he would be "not able to sin." But he fell in sin and became "not able not to sin"—that is, to always sin because of his corrupt nature. And we shared that sinful nature as his descendants. Born in Adam, we were not able not to sin. Even after we are born again, that sinful nature still remains in us as long as we live in this fallen world in our body of weakness. In Jesus Christ, we are "able not to sin" but we continue to sin and we will continue to sin until we die or Christ returns, whichever comes first. Then, only then, we will not be able to sin.

Oh, how wonderful it will be when we shall be free not only from the punishment and power of sin but also from the presence of sin altogether! Oh, how wonderful it will be when we will finally love the Lord with all of our heart, soul, mind, and strength without any distraction and hindrance, when our conscience will be free from compunction and fear, when no temptation can lure us back to our own vomit! There will be no temptation in heaven—no more tree of the knowledge of good and evil! Even if there were, temptation would lose all its power because we will be completely free from our sinful nature. Our mind will not entertain any evil thought. All this is not just wishful thinking. This is our predestined future, which cannot fail to materialize. As surely as God lives, so will this promise come to its fruition. As surely as Jesus was raised from the dead and exalted in all glory, so will we be raised in glory.

Isn't this what the last petition of the Lord's Prayer is ultimately asking for? When we enter heaven as glorified saints, then, only then, will all temptations be removed completely and all evil eradicated forever. This fact should be a great encouragement to us all. Temptations are temporary. They will not afflict us for all eternity. There will come a day when it will cease. It is not something that we have to struggle against both in this life and in the life to come. Yes, temptation will always lurk around at every step of our earthly journey, but its tenacious tentacles will not be able to reach beyond the threshold of heaven. On the other hand, Christ's salvation is eternal. The love of God will never come to an end. They are stronger than our sinfulness. They will outlast temptations and evil.

Let us live now in light of this glorious future that is ours in Jesus Christ. Let us view our life here on earth as a time of preparation for our future glory. When temptations come our way, let us conduct ourselves as those who are united with Jesus Christ. He was tempted in every respect as we are yet without sin. Let our greatest desire be to be found in Jesus Christ, now and always. Let us continue to abide in Him in order that we may not be found alone in the hour of temptation. May the word of the Lord richly dwell in us so that we may dwell in Him and abide in Him. Let us in humility pray, "Lead us not into temptation but deliver us from evil." He will not fail us. He will bring us into eternal glory.